Geist and Zeitgeist

SIX ESSAYS BY HERMANN BROCH

Geist and Zeitgeist

The Spirit in an Unspiritual Age

Edited and Introduced by John Hargraves, translator

COUNTERPOINT NEW YORK

Copyright © 2002 Suhrkamp Verlag

Library of Congress Cataloging-in-Publication Data
Broch, Hermann, 1886-1951.
  [Essays. Selections]
  Geist and Zeitgeist : six essays by Hermann Broch / introduction by
John Hargraves, translator.
    p. cm.
  ISBN 1-58243-168-X
  I. Title.
  PT2603.R657 A6 2003
  834'.912--dc21

                                                    2002006535

FIRST PRINTING

Jacket and text design by David Bullen Design

COUNTERPOINT
387 Park Avenue South
New York, NY 10016

Counterpoint is a member of the Perseus Books Group.

10 9 8 7 6 5 4 3 2 1

Contents

Introduction

SOME fifty years now after the death of Hermann Broch, it remains true that Broch's novelistic work is as well known in English, the language of his adopted country, as in German. This is only partially because of the events of history which postponed the reception of his work in Germany and Austria until after World War II. Broch's American exile lasted from 1938 until his death in 1951, and although he wrote almost exclusively in German, he spoke and corresponded in English as well and had many friends and admirers in this country. His reputation during his American exile was such that his name was mentioned for a Nobel Prize.

So it is surprising that, even now, Broch's essays are almost completely unknown to English-language readers; his reputation rests chiefly on the trilogy of novels *The Sleepwalkers,* two other novels, *The Death of Virgil* and *The Spell,* and the late cycle of stories, *The Guiltless.* Broch's essays comprise a significant portion of his total output — they fill four books of the twelve-volume edition of his works in German (letters excluded) — yet almost none of them have been translated into English. A significant exception is the translation of Broch's book-length essay *Hugo von Hofmannsthal and His Age,* by Michael P. Steinberg (University of Chicago Press, 1984), a portion of which is included in this volume.

Broch's essays span his career. They are fascinating glimpses into the mind of one of the century's most original thinkers and as free-standing essays are among the very best of any essays of the thirties and forties. However, they also provide insights into the artistic creations that Broch originally felt would replace philosophy, the utility of which he ultimately despaired of. The present volume was originally conceived as an English version of the collection *Geist und Zeitgeist,* edited by Paul Michael Lützeler, published in 1997 by Suhrkamp. This work contained five of the six essays presented here. However, I have substituted Broch's essay on translation, not present in the German collection, for a sociopolitical essay, "Human Rights and the Earthly-Absolute."[1] Some of the comments below are a compression of Lützeler's comments in his *Nachwort,* or Afterword, and some are my own.

As Lützeler remarks, theories of culture and cultural critique form the core of Broch's essayistic and literary work. The principal difference between postmodernist theories of culture and those of the modernist Broch consists in their evaluation of Western and European cultural development. Broch, like his modernist contemporaries, is still mourning the loss of cultural unity and, unlike postmodernists, cannot come to terms with the increasing pluralism of contemporary culture. Though in their examination of civilization, modernists and postmodernists both come up with the same diagnosis — i.e., the replacement of a cen-

[1.] (This essay is a chapter of the very long work on mass psychosis (*Massenwahntheorie*) which occupied Broch from 1938 to 1948. I omitted it from this collection because I think the essay should be seen in the context of the work as a whole, which is important and deserves translation in its entirety.)

tral all-determining value-set by an ever increasing number of partial systems with their own value-sets — Broch cannot find any good in this development, which he calls "the disintegration of values."

The first essay in the collection, "Evil in the Value-System of Art," analyzes a special phenomenon of cultural disintegration, kitsch, from the viewpoint not of considerations of taste, but of ethics. In doing so, the essay presents a partial view of Broch's value theory. For Broch, value theory was a complete theory of culture, which he gives at greater length in the "Disintegration of Values" portions of the *Sleepwalkers.* The great negative value of his value-system, death, stands at the center of all Broch's reflections, whether in his philosophical or in his narrative works, *The Death of Virgil* in particular. Although itself not the Absolute, death is the "gateway through which the Absolute . . . enters real life." Man's experience of the meaning of the absolute is through death, which is the impetus for man to create culture; culture is not (as in Freud) a matter of sublimating instincts, but something more basic and existential: It is man's rebellion in the face of death. To create culture is to set up the absolute of civilization, of life, in opposition to the absoluteness of death. This is a key to the moral function of art, whose effect is to undo time and thus undo man's consciousness of the ultimate negative in the universe, that is, death. This is also a key to the extremely negative role of kitsch, or imitative, non-original art; because kitsch betrays this moral function of art, it is the embodiment of evil in the value-system of art. True art is focused on a target value *(Wertziel)* of increased knowledge and perception of the universe; art has an ethical purpose and an aesthetic effect. Kitsch, or anti-art, deals in what is already known, cannot increase knowledge, and has aesthetic effect as its only goal.

The second essay, "Geist und Zeitgeist" (1934), which I have translated as "The Spirit in an Unspiritual Age," is a discussion of the significance of myth in literature and was in part prompted by Broch's reading of Joyce. Here Broch broadens his critique of culture to include the anti-religious, anti-metaphysical spirit of positivism. Symptomatic of the breakdown of a universal value-system, the growth of positivism stands in the way of a new cultural beginning. Broch sees Joyce's *Ulysses* and Mann's *Joseph* novels as hopeful signs of the rebirth of myth in the present age. The restoration of myth to literature is significant, for although "theology stands in the center of every culture, poetry stands at its beginning." Thus for Broch, restoring universal mythic values to a culture is the precondition for creating a new universal value-set; he sees myth as more than a vehicle for the cosmogony and metaphysics of primitive peoples; myth preserves humanity's Platonic primal experience, its sense of its divine origins, its knowledge of the soul. Today, the transmission and preservation of this mythic knowledge is reserved for art, which alone (as *totalitätsgestaltende Kunst*) can create an image of totality perceived as a whole.

Broch has many original insights in this essay: he laments the "muteness" of civilization stilled by the raucous competing claims of the positivistic world, a muteness that allowed "gangster" ideologies their claim on world politics and that allows philosophy to step away from its original purpose and retreat into ever smaller, increasingly irrelevant circles of supposed truth. Broch's scientific bent leads to a discussion of how a reliance on only the mathematically verifiable has brought philosophy, and the human spirit, to an impasse from which it is still struggling to extricate itself. The discussion of the deleterious effect of positivism on philosophy becomes by turns humorous, critical, and despairing, as he acknowledges the misuses to which Idealist philosophy and Nietzsche were subjected. However, the central historical dichotomy that the essay explores is that of the Spirit *(Geist)* and the Logos ("word," or the ordering principle of all human activity), an investigation that Broch starts by conflating two quotes from the Bible. Spirit and Logos are the twin driving forces of culture and history, both necessary, but Broch's implication at the end is that though the spirit is now in decline, it is the spirit for which we must continually strive, which we must keep alive.

In "James Joyce and the Current Age" (1936, translated and published in 1949 by Eugene and Maria Jolas, confidants of Joyce), Broch again urges literature to take over those questions that philosophy has abandoned and to reincorporate the mythic qualities it has lost. Only literature can give the picture of totality of today's world, which is hinted at in the range and scope of Joyce's novel *Ulysses,* a novel that gives reason to hope that through myth, a unified outlook and set of values can again be brought to civilization. Goethe's polyhistoric novel *Wilhelm Meisters Wanderjahre* is viewed as a precursor to the simultaneity and totality of scope aimed at in works such as *Ulysses* and (by implication) Broch's own *Sleepwalkers.* The essay sees in Joyce's narrative technique the influence of Einstein and Heisenberg, namely that observation itself changes what is observed: Joyce's use of language presents the narrator as both subject and object; he creates a "unity of narrated object and narrative medium."

Broch continues the discussion of myth in "Myth and the Style of Maturity" ("Mythos und Altersstil"), which he wrote twelve years later (in 1947) as an introduction to the English translation of Rachel Bespaloff's *On The Iliad.* (Bespaloff was a French professor who, like Broch, had fled Europe for New York, in 1942.) He traces myth from Homer, the threshold of myth's entrance into literature, to Tolstoy, where literature starts to become myth. Here Broch projects his own retreat from literature onto Kafka, whose attempt at mythologizing is ultimately unsuccessful, for literature is no longer in the position to create myth. Kafka transgresses the boundaries of literature, moving into a realm of untheoretical abstraction, ultimately despairing of literature and art altogether. Broch here all but abandons his earlier hope for a conflation of myth and literature *(Geist und Zeitgeist)* but suggests that a hint of the new mythology can be seen in the style of a "mature" artist (in a moment of self-reflective thought). Broch's own mature style had just been reflected in *Death of Virgil,* itself a portrait of a mature artist. This style is distinct from the "grand style" of an epoch and no longer presupposes a unity of outlook. Earlier examples of the "mature style" are found in Bach's *Art of the Fugue,* Beethoven's late quartets, and the final scenes of *Faust,* and in contemporary art, in Picasso, Stravinsky, Joyce, and Kafka. Unlike the "grand style," it is abstract, dealing with essential principles and not specific or private matters. The essay concludes with Broch's wish that the myth of the coming age, as a reaction to the pseudo-mythology of the Nazi religion, be not merely human, but humane, and in accord with the Christian tradition of the West.

I have included Broch's essay on translation (1946) partly out of my own interest in translation, but mostly because this essay shows Broch in a (perhaps) less guarded moment, delivering, in a prose even more speculative and loosely organized than his usual style, his own estimation of the effect of German language structure on German poetry. Broch subjects a well-known Romantic lyric (of Matthias Claudius) to his idiosyncratic linguistic analysis. However, this only comes after an elaborately argued and abstract discussion of the nature of symbols and symbolic language. This argument is based on a uniformity found in all human expression, a uniformity affecting both structure and content of expression. This underlying expressive meta-syntax makes translation possible, Broch argues. The central dichotomy in this essay is that between form and content, between form-based content *(geformter Inhalt)* and content-based form *(inhaltliche Formung),* the best example of the former being the languages of music and mathematics, the latter being spoken language. Broch distinguishes between German, Latin, Greek, and English, as being either sentence- and relationship-oriented languages, or fact- and word-oriented languages. The tendency of German to be ambivalent or multivalent in meaning, its false precision and breadth of meaning, its love of composite words, and its supposed "unmusicality" (despite the German genius for musical creativity) are all seen as characteristics to which the translator must be sensitive. All of these ideas are highly arguable and provocative and show the linguistic side of Broch's interests. Finally, and again provocatively, he compares the irrational, fairy-tale subconscious of German to the more rational, distinct linguistic morphology of the Latin languages and English. What is perhaps most intriguing and amusing about the entire essay is the fact that he wrote it to be delivered by his translator Jean Starr Untermeyer before a body of Yale German students as if it were her own thoughts. Although Untermeyer refused to give it, Hannah Arendt among others thought highly of the essay.

The final entry of the collection is an excerpt from Broch's book-length essay *Hugo von Hofmannsthal and His Time;* specifically it is the first chapter of the work, "Art and Its Non-Style at the End of the Nineteenth Century." Value theory is again a central concern of the essay, but the piece benefits greatly from its concreteness and wealth of detail, as it traces the cultural history of Europe (with an emphasis on the declining Habsburg empire) through the second half of the nineteenth century. The opening paragraphs throw cold water in the face of those inclined to admire the cultural achievements of that period: According to Broch, it was one of the "most wretched" eras of world history, an epoch of "falseness," of "bourgeois narrowness and pomposity." This was a period that no longer had the "grand style" of the era, but could not yet muster the strength for the "style of maturity," discussed in "Mythos und Altersstil." Instead, a "non-style" develops in the wake of competing values of "rationalism, individualism, historicism, romanticism, eclecticism, and skepticism." Opera is the representative artistic form of the period, with its overlay of art forms (as in the Wagnerian *Gesamtkunstwerk*), artificiality, and remove from reality; Vienna is a city of "museal" values; and Wagner is the artist who took most effective advantage of the "value-vacuum," the by-product of the loss of a central value-system. Wagner became a servant of the philistinism of the German public by covering up the value-vacuum, while Broch's much-admired Nietzsche attained true "epochal understanding" by recognizing and trying to overcome the negativity of the trends of his age. Using terms from the theater to describe the general cultural

environment (e.g., *Schminke* [makeup], *Dekoration*), Broch gives a cor-
rosive analysis of the flourishing "non-style" of the late nineteenth century.

The essay has much to say about myth and its place in modern culture, but even more than in his earlier essays, Broch sees literature as
failing to establish a new mythology for the new age. Instead, he again
sees Kafka as the artist coming closest (though failing to attain) this level
of literature. Broch included his own writings, *The Death of Virgil* in
particular, as a forerunner (and not as the fulfillment) of this mythic literature.

The final chapter of the excerpt, the title of which, "The Gay
Apocalypse," has become a watchword on its own, is a brilliant picture
of the epicenter of this value-vacuum, Broch's own city of Vienna. It is
among the best things Broch the essayist wrote, moving from comparisons of Vienna with Paris, to descriptions of the Habsburg monarchy
in a time of increasing democratic and constitutional pressures, its politics of "parrying" and its pleasure-seeking, careless aristocracy, its pre-
Hitlerian anti-Semitism, its centrifugal nationalist tendencies that ultimately tore the monarchy apart, ending in Broch's verdict of Vienna as
the "metropolis of kitsch," as the capital of the value-vacuum.

It is hoped that the appearance of these six essays together in one
volume will result in a wider appreciation of the intellectual depth and
cultural range of Broch's thought.

John Hargraves

G&Z

Evil in the Value-System of Art *(1933)* [1]

translated by John Hargraves

I. THE PROBLEM

IF IN the course of civilization it was always art and its respective styles that gave most visible expression to the lifestyles of different epochs, and if this applies as well to the present time, then art would make particularly manifest the extreme nature of the current period; our time places the highest ethical demands on humanity and its capacity for self-sacrifice; despite such clearly ethical striving, it is a time filled with horror, bloodlust, and injustice; and, moreover, it can dismiss all this so lightly — all this would have to be made manifest in art. Art would also show that this time is striving toward a new spiritual and Platonic union with an intensity unheard of for centuries, but that it is nonetheless mired in positivistic thinking, in an obsession with the factual, which abhors everything that is Platonic or deductive and which stands in odd

[1.] Hermann Broch, "Das Böse im Wertsystem der Kunst," *Schriften zur Literatur 2: Theorie* (Frankfurt am Main: Suhrkamp, 1975), pp. 119–57.

contrast to its ethical striving. Can art really give expression to all this? Is it up to such a task?

And more than this, is art still capable of resolving such problems at all? Is it not precisely the tendency of ethics (to whose new rigor mankind is now subject) to oppose all art and all artistic practice, to the point that it would be an absurdity if this new lifestyle were expressed in any style of art? Is it not precisely characteristic of a radically de-Platonized world, a positivistic world, to relegate any esthetic considerations to the sphere of philosophical pseudo-problems, as radically as it rejects anything metaphysical? Even the previous era, that prewar period we call the "bourgeois" era, surely did not find its expression in the eclectic styles that it produced, and if it had any kind of representative art, it was that of grand opera only; and if art had a kind of intellectual and social status, art and the concern with art became primarily an interest of otherwise idle ladies of the bourgeois class. And although a purification process has begun since then, which in a certain sense reflects the world's new ethical rigor and which has created at least in architecture a pronounced style for the age *(Zeitstil),* the interest in these artistic problems remains confined to the circle of those immediately concerned, has become, so to speak, an internal discussion among artists; a development that had begun in the nineteenth century now became clearly apparent: The obvious expression of the age is far more visible in machine technology or sports events than in urban architecture or works of art.

It would be all too easy simply to maintain that intellectual and esthetic problems have been ignored because they are essentially concerns that have been overwhelmed by the most pressing current question: "Do we have enough to eat?" No, this one-sided materialistic view is contradicted by the fact that it was the Middle Ages, a period of the most intense material deprivation, that produced the most sublime works of art, and even easier to assert the cliché that in any case the Muses are silent in times of war, for even this view is repeatedly disproven by history — all this would be too easy, would lead, if one may say so, to a lopsided pathology of the time. For although war may have been the great catalyst, bringing all the developing forces into literally explosive acceleration, and although war itself may be seen as the result of catastrophic economic or technical development, even perhaps of scientific and intellectual development, all these phenomena, however much they may mutually explain, cause, and even intensify one another, are nonetheless closely related sets of symptoms of a single colossal logical process. This process, occurring over hundreds of years, is one in which the European worldview, first formed by the Middle Ages, was dissolved bit by bit, and in which the individual value-systems became independent from one another, but in which man, increasingly confused and torn by both destructive and constructive forces, has lost the ability to halt the final disintegration of the old given values, to hold off the final bloody chaos, and finds himself to an increasing degree at the mercy of his own conscience, in the face of horror and death still confronted with the question, like a thunderclap: "What should we do?" And this question resounds wherever mankind attempts to be equal to the demands and needs of the time; everywhere its ethical urgency erupts with a vehemence that implies that the question "Do we have enough to eat?" can only be resolved in ethical, not material, terms.

For the collapse of the material-economic field of values can only be understood in the context of the collapse of a comprehensive general value-system. This state of affairs is now known to all: It is obvious, and intuitively so, that the hiatus between "no more" and "not yet," this intermediary stage, in which the confusion of decline joins with the confusion of quest, forms the starting point of a new spiritual union; from this, only now, can we re-clarify rational definitions about value and nonvalue. Even with positivism's abhorrence of speculative and theological definitions, with its preference for nonspeculative, emotionally grounded, and intuitively justifiable values, this goal is an unmistakably Platonic one, for it must culminate in a rational value-system, in which the world's plausibility, reason, and values will acquire new, systematic grounding. Despite philosophy's low esteem in the eye of the practical man as well as the scientist, we should take due note that the current worldwide renaissance of interest in Nietzsche has a symptomatic significance, not so much on account of its new moral content (for Nietzsche, a product of his time, is grounded in a bourgeoisie more tuned to esthetics) but rather because of the demands he made of method and principle, where he made the concept of value the methodological heart of philosophy; it was an almost impassioned insight into the as-yet-unforeseeable implications of the concept of value that moved Nietzsche (and Kierkegaard as well), and, however hesitantly, however reluctantly the various schools of philosophy, whether Neo-Kantian or otherwise, adopted the concept of value, they really had no choice; everything clearly indicates that it was just this value-concept that had so suddenly come to the fore which enabled them to build a bridge between a foundering and outmoded speculative philosophy and the possibility of a new metaphysics. The enormous tension between good and evil, the intense polarity of paired opposites that characterizes our age and gives it its specifically extremist nature, this compulsion for people to incorporate into their lives both the highest ethical needs and an often incomprehensibly frightful reality, so that life can be lived at all — all this gives direction to the intellectual strivings of the age, gives its struggles a legitimization that it had seemingly lost.

And this is also the point where art, its social esteem notwithstanding, makes its relevance felt anew as a representative phenomenon of the time, and where it again becomes a genuine problem of the age; the problem of art itself has become an ethical one. Not only have poetry and the fine arts too become more and more tendentious in their attempt, whether didactic or satirical, to express the ethical character of the age, but that very polarity of good and evil has become quite plainly evident in art itself. If we speak of art's loss of relevance, we have in mind only the one pole, that of the good, that is, that conception of art as it was understood, rightly, through the centuries. For in times of securely held values, it is easy to separate out evil from individual value-fields (easier than in the present age, which has declined into a value-anarchy), easier even though the tension between the poles of good and evil was considerably smaller. One knew what was meant by art: good art. Today there also is good art, that is, that art which in its purest state is under the rule of the ethical, but this forms just one part of the value-field called "art," and this isolated part, whether it succeeds in creating its own style of art or not, is still not an expression of the lifestyle of the world or the age. One sees this most clearly, perhaps, in music, which in many respects is now undergoing a process of renovation,[2] but whose influence and effect in general is becoming ever narrower, while at the same time a music industry of undreamt-of dimensions has taken hold throughout the world. Along with music as an art in the sense we have meant till now, kitsch-music has appeared, and when we speak of the artistic expression of the age, without doubt this negative pole is more significant than the positive one of genuine art. Or, more correctly: The artistic expression of the age is to be seen in the enormous tension between good and evil within art. For the evil in art is kitsch.

There is probably no place where the restructuring of value-standards, where the effective reach of evil in the world is so pronounced as in the existence of kitsch, which, significantly, is an offspring of the bourgeois age, and first appears precisely when the world entered into an age where its intellectual content converged with its actual appearance, that is, the Machine Age; at the same time its positivistic tendencies intensified into a most rigorous materialism. And precisely because a positivist, anti-Platonic world has been forced to choose the principle "Beauty is what pleases us," not just as a convenient and to

[2.] Broch is referring to serial music. Cf. his essay on Schönberg: "Zum Problem der Erkenntnis in der Musik." Broch's reference to "a music industry of undreamt-of dimensions" reflects his awareness of the growth of a mass market for popular music in film, radio, and the recording industry.

some extent theoretical formula, but rather as a rule to live by — for this reason it appears particularly to be the special function of kitsch (though it represents only a part of art's total product) to embody art's old task, to be the manifest expression of the age. But to understand how this partial value-area can become the symbol of a comprehensive value-setting system, how the ethical makeup of the time can be seen to appear in the esthetic phenomenon of kitsch, one must understand what constitutes the concept of values in general.

II. The Construct of Values: Overcoming Death

The countenance of death is the great awakener! Nietzsche's experience in the French infirmaries of 1870, those events of war that had a decisive or at least accelerating effect on his development, fifty years later took on an infinitely greater dimension; in that Europe of fifty years later, death had become the somber sovereign of all things, and the horror of death cried out to the heavens: Only then had the collapse of all values become apparent, fear of the loss of all life's values descended upon mankind, and the fearful question as to the possibility of a new value-construct became inevitable.

To be sure, a world turned to positivism must deal with the reality of death with the same heroic realism with which it deals with all other manifestations of life. That era of rising positivism, the Renaissance, made the brashly hopeful attempt (perhaps condemned to fail for just this reason) to overcome death by its openly sensual, "pagan" affirmation of life. But at the same time a Protestantism arose filled with ascetic tendencies, to convert with its new rigor life's chaotic anxieties into new values and attitudes. For even though the immediacy of death may force us to look it in the eye, even though its threatening proximity may narrow the focus of this anxiety to a fear that can be deflected like the danger that gave rise to it — all the same, death remains concealed in a world of night and uncertainty, and in this darkness fear resides, and against this uncertainty of darkness, this fear born of an isolation that accompanies a man's soul from the moment he opens his eyes to consciousness until that moment when he closes them for eternity, against this fear there is no possible defense, no way to numb its impact: The human soul's task is to secure itself, to protect itself against this fear.

Everything that we know as "value" and which deserves that name aims at the nullification and overcoming of death. Death is the opposite of value, it is un-value *a priori*, seen in opposition to the value of life, even when it can only be overcome by itself, when it is death that overcomes death, when death itself is transformed into a life-value, by linking the two infinities in a circle, in the ultimate sense of a redemption through death. And because the eternity of death is the gateway, the only gateway through which the absolute enters into real life in all its magical meaningfulness, bringing in its train the magic words "infinity," "eternity," and "universe," words that otherwise could not withstand logical analysis, and because death in its unimaginable remoteness from life is nonetheless so near to life that it continuously fills the human soul with its physical presence and its metaphysical existence — because of death, the only absolute of reality and of nature, another absolute must be thrown up against it by the human will, which can create the absolute of the soul and the absolute of civilization; and this remarkable ability of the soul, perhaps the most amazing phenomenon of human existence, finds its form of expression in that ever-renewing act, which could simply be called the "act of being human," and in this humanity, human existence is elevated to the act of value setting and value creating.

Epistemological Comment

Value is a concern of empirical life. Not the empirical life of the man in the street, but of a category that one could call the Platonic idea of empirical life.

In the category of pure consciousness, which philosophy normally deals with, there is no such thing as value, indeed, there is not even the concept of truth, or that of thought which creates truth, for pure consciousness is timeless like God, it does not need to "develop," either from untruth to truth, or from evil to good, or least of all from value to "nonvalue." It is one of the antinomies of all theologies that God needs the world to create himself.

But this absolute isolation, this autonomy of God and of pure consciousness has nonetheless become part of the "Platonic idea of empirical humanity," it is a fact that the soul, filled with fear, experiences constantly; it is the desperate isolation of the human being dying alone. Whatever appears to the ego as value is based directly or indirectly upon this isolation, which is as near to and as far from death as death is near to and far from life, and so the absoluteness of life's value, which is opposed to the absoluteness of death, is also a condition of this isolation, precisely as this isolation is constantly at work in all acts of value setting, is seen in them and lends all created things their peculiar character of autonomy, by which the Ego itself is characterized.

Isolation is the logical commonality of humankind and God. But if man distinguishes between himself and God — and he does — if empirical consciousness is to be distinguished from consciousness *per se,* then the idea of time and also the idea of relativity must be enlisted. The concept of truth remains void as long as the concept of untruth is not associated with it, indeed, it would remain void if there were not varying gradations of truth. And the ethical character of truth, its impatient and demanding teleological character, would be empty if there did not exist a category (unimaginable in the realm of pure consciousness) that has the power to rank itself higher than truth, to make this truth become what it in fact is in real life: a "value" among life's other values.

In other words, in the sphere of pure consciousness, insofar as one can speak of truth at all, thought has primacy over life, the primacy of *cogito* over *sum,* the primacy of the category of truth over that of value.

In the realm of empirical life, this relationship is reversed; here the primacy rightly goes to life, with all its emotional variety and all its irrationality, here truth is a value among other values, the category of value is dominant. And if this empirical ego is able to uncover even merely relative truths, it remains in its autonomy and its aloneness permanently at the stage of a more or less subjective absoluteness: It cannot lie to itself, it finds itself at every instant of its existence in a state, if one can put it thus, of "maximal truth," but it finds itself as well at every instant in a "state of maximal value"— and no matter how it acts, it creates in its isolation from moment to moment the most favorable value situation for itself, and only retroactively does it conceive of the prior, just-transpired situation as non-truth, as nonvalue, as error to be rejected.

The Dual Aspect of Value: Ethical and Esthetic

In the realm of the empirical, truth is subordinate to a more general category, that of value. Truth becomes a value among other values, which exist with the same claim for validity as itself. And it is clear that even the truth-producing acts, acts of thought, in short, thinking, lose their unique *a priori* privileged position, are degraded to a kind of action, differing from other value-creating acts only in that they bring the "truth," instead of other values, into being; thinking becomes a special case of action in general, of value-setting activity, since in the autonomy of the ego there exist only acts aimed at value.

But all activity is formative, there is no empirical or ideal activity whose aim is not to form or re-form objective reality. Every activity of mankind is formative, and the world it creates, to become part of the world, and to undo death, arises from Anaximander's *apeiron* (unknowable), from the primal cause *(Urgrund)* of the amorphic, from the irrational *per se,* in whose "quality-less-ness" life and death, nonbeing and being are united and still formless. The creation of values is a path that leads always from the unformed to the formed, or at least the better-

formed, and that which is unformed or less formed is always the irrational; in its darkness, the irrational, wherever and however it appears,
cannot be distinguished from the darkness of death; it carries death
within itself, and to shape the irrational, to cast light upon it, illuminates
death, illuminates a piece of the future snatched from death, becomes
known, finally becomes something rational and visible in the world —
and in a world that has a formed and conceptual rationality, a rationality
in which value can be constituted.

Nowhere is this so clearly apparent as in the phenomenon of time:
not physical time, but that time which is man's most basic experience of
life, that time which ebbs away in every hour of his breathing, conducts
him into the future and ends in death. In time and its passing, the relativity of values is anchored, the eternal reminder that human value setting cannot escape relativity as it aspires to divine absoluteness. Thus,
the goal of all formative activity is to create simultaneity out of the
sequentiality of values, to create a value-system in which individual
values no longer succeed one another individually and in sequence, but
which support one another in common. It is this transformation of tem-
poral sequence into a construct that must be termed "spatial" in an
expanded sense, and that, to the last detail, reflects the value-system of
music — the transformation of sequential to simultaneous, perceived
spatially: This is the essence of music.

So if the concept of "form" is defined widely enough, then one could
say all human action aims at forming an object, an object that exists in
space. It is certainly not just a terminological convention, but rather the
generally understood sense of the words, to say that formative acts are
the concern of ethical valuation and that the results of these formative
acts are the concern of esthetic valuation. And since all human actions
and their results are values, it follows that within a given set of values,
ethical valuation and esthetic valuation are closely coordinated; in the
framework of any given or accepted value-set, every action that can be
termed ethical, thus "good," brings about an esthetically positive result,

and every result that this brings about, that can be valued as esthetically positive, thus "beautiful," points to a prior ethically positive act, and the same is true if we put the terms in the negative.

The old coordination of "good" and "beautiful" is only logically meaningful within a general concept of value that includes both, given a particular set of values; on the other hand, logically the concept of value is sufficiently constituted only in this double aspect, in this dynamic-static dichotomy—the ethical creating of value, and the esthetic value result.

This means that within the empirical world, and thus in history too (for the empirical world is in time and thus in history), the esthetic is the ethical become reality. Remembering the extraordinary role of the concept of value, not just in philosophical-historical considerations but in history itself (history being the world's verdict on itself),[3] one may then deduce from the esthetic residuals of history the ethical deeds that are preserved for eternity solely in their esthetic legacy.

Autonomy and Absolute Nature of Value

That absolute quality required of all values and every value-system is a projection of the autonomous ego. Into every value and every value-system a value-setting subject is projected, latently or openly, a "god" who creates value. The system attains this godlike absoluteness only if all the phenomenal world is subject to the formative, value-setting will, only when all values share a common system, representing collectively an esthetic value in the widest sense, such that life's irrationality in all its breadth and depth is transformed into rational truth, rational form.

This pan-rationalism, the goal of the total system in its claim to absolute authority, becomes a kind of mathematical image of this absolute, for the infinite nature of the world as a whole, which is recalled by

---

3. "Die Weltgeschichte ist das Weltgericht."

values, is subject to number; number's infinity is "all," and we are concerned here with "all" values that can be gathered into a complete system; a hierarchy must extend over "all" world values, if conversely it is to take on the authority of the absolute — that is, the absolute quality of the great world religions, which grow up in this way; as one saw in the medieval Western Christian/Platonic worldview, this organon of values, in its claim to totality was the "only way to salvation," with the result that at the time of its full sway it represented the nearest approach to an absolute liberation from death.

But at this point of nearest approach to the absolute, every value-system, no matter how powerful, must begin the process of self-renewal. For the absolute will always be unattainable, and every step toward reaching it will always be followed by yet another, even closer approximation. Each and every Platonic system must finally concede that it cannot cover "all" values or contents in the world; every form of Platonism must be resolved to positive and positivistic empirical experience, and even at the cost of their own dialectic self-dissolution they must necessarily strive toward self-renewal.

For the West, this dialectic self-dissolution came about with the Protestant division of the Church, and this retroactive dissolution of an integral value-system into ever smaller systems, each one of which, in turn autonomous and laying claim to exclusive validity and absolute authority, ended in that fearful anarchy of values and mutual incomprehension in which the struggle of individual value-systems concludes in violence and death, an anarchy in which the Platonic Idea appears to be extinguished utterly, giving way to the unspiritual *per se*.

Rational Formation and Irrational Goal

The larger the system, the more difficult it is to define rationally. Its rationality is visible only in its esthetic result, in the visible church, in the totality of its dogmas, in what already has real form. But if we ask about the goal of the value-system *(Wertziel des Systems),* it remains indefinable. For the very smallest systems and for individual values an ultimate goal can be given: The value-goal of the shoemaker or the tailor is rationally perceptible, but the value-goal of large systems remains indefinable and irrational, since it is infinite, and remains infinitely removed, be it called "God," "the people," "beauty," or "justice."

And yet the God who is introduced into every value-system arrives with certain ethical demands on mankind, commanding, "Thou shalt act in such and such a way, and thou wilt be immortal," adding, "Thou shalt have no other value-systems beside me." What value-aim does he reveal to humanity, if he cannot define it?

Now it is true that every value-system represents a hierarchy of values, but also that the ultimate value standing at the apex of the hierarchy, by reason of internal logic, cannot itself be part of the system; it is only represented by the system: "Science" as such is an empty concept, only gaining meaning as the totality of all scientific actions and methods. The goal remains in the irrationality of the future, and only when the future is given form and illumination can this goal itself be made clear.

In accordance with this remarkable state of affairs, the medieval artist did indeed keep his eye fixed exclusively on the infinite value-aim of the system, that is, God — but he could only serve God by producing well-crafted handiwork. God was not his problem, even if the things he was painting were symbols of God; the problems he needed to solve were not in God, but in the colors and spatial layouts, the people and animals whom he painted to honor God. And the silversmiths and shoemakers, the linen weavers, all did just the same — each performing his earthly labor for its own sake, keeping only in his mind's eye the remote goal that gave earthly endeavors their ethical direction. But even the Church itself was prone to skepticism toward anyone whose work was focused all too directly on God; indeed, it quickly sensed in such attitudes a whiff of heresy. Man was to live by dogma, he was expected to subjugate himself to the "technique" of the Church, if we can say it that way; but beyond that he was expected to fulfill his ethical obligation as a Chris-tian, i.e., to serve God exclusively by performing his earthly labor for the sake of the work alone. And it was only in the context of all these attitudes that he acted truly ethically; only through the accumulation of all ethical acts — of which each one, as we said, brought about an esthetic result, if only a partial result—would he attain the final esthetic result, which was located in the infinite; only thus would he reach the supra-esthetic goal, the state of grace and eternal bliss. But this ultimate effect played no role in the creation of the painter's picture, the armorer's sword, or the cobbler's shoe.

Although art is no longer a part of the religious system, having become autonomous like all other value-systems since the breakup of that all-encompassing system of religion, reinforcing this autonomy with the principle of *l'art pour l'art,* nonetheless, art even today has set down its own private theology in a series of aesthetic theories, and continues to hold to its highest value-goal, and this, too, continues to hover in the realm of the infinite, be it called "beauty," "harmony," or whatever else. And the ethical demand made of the artist is, as always, to produce "good" works, and only the dilettante and the producer of kitsch (whom we meet here for the first time) focus their work on beauty.

For the esthetic in general as an expression of the supreme ultimate value of a system can influence the result of ethical action only secondarily, just as "wealth" is not the main goal but the side effect of individual commercial activity. And "wealth" itself is an irrational concept. It is an almost mystical process, the setting of ethical values: Arising from the irrational, transforming the irrational to the rational, yet nonetheless it is the irrational that radiates from within the resulting form.

III. The Irrational in
the Construct of Values

The Subjective Element in Value Creation

But what does this mean, to demand that art produce works that are "good," rather than "beautiful"? Although it may not be easy to articulate a general formula, it still seems certain that "good" work must be in accord with the idea of autonomy peculiar to every value-system. And since value and truth are very closely allied in this idea of autonomy, so much so that the autonomous development of the value-system bears the stamp of an inner truth, then one can surely maintain that truth in a work of art has a significance one always felt intuitively: "Good" work must be able to connect in a certain way to the epistemological nature of art, to the discovery of new insights and new forms of seeing and experiencing that confer the character of universal truth not just to fine arts or to literature but to the entire range of art. This always concerns, even in music, the portrayal of an inner or an outer world, a representation that must, first of all, be unmediated, and therefore unswervingly truthful. We are dealing here with a kind of "expanded naturalism," in which van Gogh and Kafka would deserve inclusion as much as Dürer and Zola. It is always a question of showing the (inner or outer) world "as it really is."

But if one can in fact see or sense in this expanded naturalism the mystical irrationality of the final value-goal, then this is not simply "showing the world as it really is." Here forces must be at work that go beyond this prescription. And in fact it is evident that along with the naturalistic tendency there exists another tendency, no less strong, to "show the world as one wishes or fears it to be." In other words, along with the objective condition of the first demand there is a subjective condition that probably constitutes a personal prerequisite for all artistic creativity, and all artistic enjoyment. No matter how naturalistic, literature will scarcely want to dispense with the victorious hero, or to do without the hero defeated only after attaining inner victory; it is basically unimportant whether the desire to create and enjoy art arises from simple identification with such heroes, or if the primitive artist was undergoing some rudimentary and magical process of fear-exorcism, or yielding to some metaphysical impulse, when he painted his hunting-scenes on the walls of his cave: What the naïve man (and not only he) finds "beautiful" in a work of art is the result of these subjective, affective pleasures, of a very personal liberation from fear, uniting him with the infinite and irrational final value-goal in a literal *unio mystica.*

The Vocabulary of Reality in the Syntax of the Value-Set

Now it is quite unlikely that this mystical connection is confined to relationships of this type, i.e., ones simply based on subject matter, for only a small portion of art is based on the reproduction and representation of subject matter, a process that excludes music and many other areas; moreover, one can also assume that similar conditions likewise apply to the other value-systems. All those who do work that sets values lay claim to a certain "artistry" separating them from the mere bureaucrat; and this is justly so: The great statesman, the great general, the great merchant, all pursue their activities in some ways "artistically."

If we object that the merchant, the general, the statesman impact the world directly, while art manufactures mere images, one could answer that art, too, undertakes to create forms directly from materials such as paint, tones, words, stone, and concrete, so that here too we speak not of original creation, but likewise a transformation, a re-forming. Of course this is beside the point, for basically these materials are merely auxiliary. The actual material that art works with and turns into works of art one could describe as "vocabulary units of reality" *(Realitätsvo- kabel).* Poetry, for example, does not arbitrarily string words together (except in

Dadaism), but rather sets up specific situations: "A man crosses the street" would be a kind of vocabulary unit of reality. Even the most fantastic and unreal poetry consists of such units. Nor are matters different in the other arts; even in music such vocabulary units of reality can be found.

But what are individual actions in a battle? What are individual political actions? What are individual commercial transactions? From this viewpoint, they are surely nothing but vocabulary units of reality, and if the handling of these vocabulary units can be considered artistry, then the "selection" made to create from them a new scheme of values is a function of the "creative license" that the artist, and all who call themselves artists, lays claim to.

Of course this creative license is not without limits: It has a close connection with the autonomy of the value-system in which it operates: The Christian's freedom is the freedom of God, and is dependent on him. And just as one cannot string words together without heeding the value-system of language, just as it is impossible to use those words outside of the prescribed linguistic syntax, it is just as impossible to break the bonds of the specific syntax inherent in any value-system. The value-systems of politics, of military strategy, of commerce, all have their specific syntactic regulations, from which the agreed-upon values of the value-system get their particular significance: It is the actual "systemic idea" by which every value-system is governed, and just as the position of a word in the sentence not only colors the specific meaning of the word but changes the sense of the sentence, so also the position of the vocabulary units of reality in the value-system depends on this productive reciprocity.

The affinity of art to dreams has often been pointed out, and even dreams make use of the vocabulary units of reality that they take from the external world and that constitute, so to speak, the dream's objective existence. Dreams also have syntactic laws, according to which the vocabulary units are generally used. But in applying these laws, the dreamer is allowed much subjective, "creative" freedom: the same creative freedom with which artistic people handle syntax in every value-system.

The energy formed in words and lines, this quiet lending of meaning which is realized through selective use of these vocabulary units of reality, and which constitutes the essence of poetry, is at the same time the system's driving idea, and the power of this syntax can be so great, as in lyric poetry, that a single one of these units of reality can light up the whole world. For by virtue of poetic syntax, this unit of reality connects with all others in the world, all the others are intuitively felt in this one, and poetry's ultimate value, cosmic limitlessness, is fulfilled in the single reality-unit of a lyric poem.

The Example of Music

Music, the art most deeply linked to the emotions, yet nonetheless the most rational, expresses its syntax most purely and clearly through the laws of counterpoint. And nowhere else is it so clear as precisely here, in music's rational and visible syntax; all its discipline notwithstanding, music remains the production of a creative subject, a personal creativity that is as irrational as the person who performs it; truly, if all art is a representation of the world, here an inner world, if music, with ever more complex counterpoint, could ultimately represent the inner world of a Beethoven, and the mystical archetype that all music has as its ultimate, infinite goal, then it represents also an absolute redemption from death — the aim of all creativity, and which the value-system as a whole promotes.

The Irrational and Conservative in the Work of Art

Here the function of the value-system of art in contrast to the function of the other value-systems is revealed — the former has the enormous and near magical advantage that in every act it makes, it does not just hint at but actually reflects that totality.

But this reflection of the final, irrational value-goal, this reflection of totality gives the work of art another special significance: For every "unclosed" value-system — for example, the system of science — the esthetic concretization of its ethical efforts is already outdated and over-taken at the very moment of occurrence. Any given state of science is usually made obsolete at the very moment it is reached, becoming at that moment the object of re-forming again; one could even say that what has already been formed takes on once again the character of the unformed. In the work of art, what "was," the esthetic result of ethical impulse, is the unmediated image of the future toward which it is striving; this claim to totality is reflected in every individual artwork, and this closed qual-ity, the quality of being "at rest in itself" which is the hallmark of the true work of art, this being lifted out of time, this value scheme made con-crete in itself, can surely be understood as the second major reason for the dominant position of art throughout history.

And probably this is also why the artwork, and the esthetic in general, has been assigned such a significant role in every conservative value-system. For the future harbors darkness and death, and the only safety that life offers is in the visible and the created, thus ultimately in the past, and it is consistent with the absolutist tendency of value creation that there is also one value-system — the conservative system — that would likewise make into absolutes these values of a preformed past. But the artwork already represents this quality of the absolute. Indeed, it bears the mirror image of this absoluteness within itself, and one could almost say that art, in contradistinction to science, which in its structure is rev-olutionary and absolutely committed to progress, needs always to be conservative (although, in a peculiar, but probably necessary dialectic reversal, the individual artist is generally revolutionary, while the scien-tist is usually conservative). And if as it develops, art is continually mindful of what has been, if (art theories being in constant flux) the Renaissance and Classicism recalled ancient Greece and Rome, while Romanticism turned to the Gothic, then such phases in the develop-ment of a style of life are not only a general and necessary phenomenon, but in such constant and inextinguishable continuity of events one finds perhaps the strongest possible case for the unity of civilization, for a totality of what is human, a totality that encompasses all times and regions of the earth, expressing simultaneously the closed nature of the artwork and the claim to totality of the creative human being.

For everything conservative goes back as well to the irrationality of man, and if we call the conservative maintenance of old values and attitudes "Romanticism," then it is an essential component of this Romanticism to locate its sense of the world not in rational thought but in human feeling, in the intuitions and premonitions of the blood. And that remarkable merging of past and future that is characteristic of the search for values acquires a coloration that directly connects the human, irrational experience of values with the cosmos, with the final value-goals of humanity: the mysteries of blood and sexuality but also those mysteries of art — insofar as they mean the Dionysian-creative — that closeness to death that is a part of the fearful existence of every creature becomes simultaneously the way the supreme value releases us from death. It is an arch spanning the irrationality of the past to the irrationality of the future, rising out of fear, and reaching toward fear, yet taking with it the dark knowledge of life into the darkness of death, projecting back into its origin a final defeat of death, which is its aim; a gleam of light between two darknesses, the artwork is the symbol of being and of eternity, and a constant deliverance from fear.

IV. Nonvalue

Nonvalue as Defining Element for Every Value-System

The establishment of value-systems occurs as a result of ethical demand; this demand specifies how the person belonging to the system must conduct himself, in order to share in the final value-goal.

But the very impossibility of defining the value-goal in its infinite nature has shown that an ethical demand is merely a kind of direction giving, that it would be wrong to expect specific individual regulations. Every demand is based on an action, and just as every action is fixed between two stationary poles, and moves back and forth from one to the other, and can only be defined when these two things are known, the same applies to every demand made of such actions: It can only be defined when the two stationary poles, the point of origin and the destination point of the action, are known. Where this is not the case, where, as in every value-system, only the point of origin lies within the real and the visible, and moreover, all that is known is that actions that are a part of the system move away from this point of origin, for the entire system is occupied in a continuous evolution, striving toward the infinite — then the ethical demand can no longer consist of the "finite" formulation "Thou shalt strive toward this or that finite Goal," but can only be put negatively: "Thou shalt quit this momentary and visible condition."

And it is in fact true that all ethical imperatives in the world of the empirical, which is where they acquire moral character, appear in negative form. Seven of the Ten Commandments have the form "Thou shalt not," and the other three can easily be shown to be derivatives of absolutes. A book of laws is always a collection of prohibitions. And no matter how many "Thou shalt nots" are set down, the goal that fits all these prohibitions is not defined but is only approximated in endless circles.

So if the value-system actually consists of ethical demands that the values of the system must satisfy, this not only points to the permanently open quality of its constitution and definition but also lends it the general structure of "Thou shalt not," which always originates in the visible, definable, in what already has form, and so can be ultimately repudiated. No value could exist at all, if the "Thou shalt not" did not proceed from a nonvalue, from an evil, which is definable and at the same time repudiated. Value is constituted by nonvalue, the value-system is constituted by the evil that it overcomes, from which it develops continually, the evil that in the end always means death.

Nonvalue: Function of the Autonomy of Value

But here too there exists the same interaction, because the evaluation of what must be deemed value or nonvalue, as bad or good, is controlled by the system; the "bad" from which the value-system is supposedly constituted is not absolute, but, due to the relativity of values, is a function of the system. To create saleable mass-produced goods is an ethical value for the mercantile system, but for the artistic system, a nonvalue.

So if the constitution of nonvalue is to be separated from the relativity of a plurality of differing given value-systems, then it must be based on the structure of the systems themselves. And once again we must deal with autonomy, for the defining characteristic of every value-system is its aspiring to the absolute: Every value-system, indeed every individual value itself claims to be uniquely valid *a priori* and in a way would claim all one's available consciousness (the psychology of children and primitive peoples would provide plenty of examples), and only through the necessities of practical life are groups and hierarchies of values built that finally mature into unified systems. But whatever remains outside the system, both in theory and in fact, can never take on the character of value, it remains nonvalue, perhaps neutral to the system, but only so long as no direct contact with the system itself takes place. For that menacing, dark, and incomprehensible quality, which is always obscurely the reality of death, this quality is attached to every alien system (even while still neutral), but as soon as it abandons its neutrality and enters into logical connection with one's own system, it is immediately actualized, it becomes evil, and leads to a war of opposing values.

Evil in Dogmatism

Although the struggle of individual value-systems is real and plainly raging all about us, our concept of it is nonetheless entirely anthropomorphic; it is a kind of war of the gods, a war between imaginary subjects of commercial, military, national, or other systems. And the logical connection between two value-systems that is required to transform the neutral alien value into "evil" is seen to some extent as the intrusion of one god on the ethical authority of another. This intervention, which the autonomous freedom of one system is supposed to suffer at the hands of another, is an impairment of that "freedom" which is so closely connected with the system's autonomy. It does not matter if this impairment consists of commands that art be patriotic, that military operations be conducted in accordance with the views of the aristocracy, or that a capitalist economy allow socialist viewpoints to prevail, it is always this breach of its autonomy that is felt by a value-system to be "evil." The formulation of evil as a breach in a system's autonomy is independent of the content or nature of the particular value-system; it is a condition of its structure only, and if the breach of a value-system's autonomic authority can be called the essence of dogmatism, then dogmatism is "evil" *per se.*

Nonetheless, the necessary logical connection has not yet been established. The dogmatic attack on a system by some alien system can of course actually occur under certain circumstances, but there is always a degree of arbitrariness about it, and as such says nothing about the logical possibility or the structure of such an attack. For even if the origin of the dogmatic, the origin of evil, must be displaced onto an alien system, if it must always need to come from an "outside," a realm of darkness and death, where one's "own" values do not apply, there must still exist certain logical preconditions that enable the alien system to carry out this attack, and we must at a minimum assume that in the alien system certain phenomena that are considered "good" in one's own system are considered "evil," for without this presupposition no attack on one's own ethical postulates could take place. So it is always a certain dialectic relationship, a dialectic process of divergence, which must be present in part or in full between the two warring value-systems: What is considered good in the one must be evil in the other. This type of systemic pair is well known: One could actually speak of "oppositional systems," theism-atheism, capitalism-socialism, militarism-pacifism, to name a few examples.

Thus, independent of whether the "evil" in fact attacks from an empirically opposed outside system, or whether it has developed dialectically from within one's own system (for there exists no value-system from whose values and attitudes the "criminal" opposition could not be logically derived), the "valuation" that the valuating subject performs in his own system is always such that the subject isolates evil as an oppositional value, locating it in an external and criminal oppositional system, which is then held responsible for the dogmatic attack.

The historical process in which human life is played out collectively or individually is an aggregate of innumerable value-systems, and regardless of whether the systems coexist in mutual indifference or whether they overlap, support, or oppose one another, an individual by his actions can belong to the most diverse value-systems but remains compelled to unite these different impulses into a single system of his own, to make them to some extent a part of his personal biology. The more polarized the world and its value-systems become, the greater and more painful the tension is between them, the more difficult it becomes for the individual psyche to cope with the values of good and evil imposed upon it. Man always sins with only one part of his being. But when this balance of values is disturbed, when he transgresses against the complex value-system comprising "society," its value-system then goes into action and "expels" him; he is then relegated into an opposing system, the "criminal" system dialectically opposed to the system of society, for it is presumed that he has acted according to the laws of this opposing system.

Radical Evil in the Imitation System

So far as verbal definition is allowable, the difference between radical evil and criminal evil is the "non-excludability" of radical evil; when

Savonarola burned paintings and thus acted against the value-system of art, the motivation for his actions was located in a value-system of religion and asceticism; when an enemy army invades a country, it acts according to its own native system; when the Convention felt compelled to sentence Louis XVI to death, it did indeed offend the monarchic value-system but acted within the value-system of freedom; for each value-system that is "offended," an externally located oppositional system can be given, to which responsibility for such actions can be ascribed, and as long as this can be done, the evil remains within the relativity of the value-system; call it "error," call it "simple evil," or even "criminality," but the boundary separating it from "absolute evil" has not yet been crossed. But when such an "outside" force, aimed at the destruction of the system and the abolition of its values, is no longer to be found, when destruction becomes self-destruction, arising from and using the means of the system itself, a self-destruction that cannot be excused as "seduction" from without, then it is appropriate to speak of the effect of "radical evil." Radical evil is innate within the system and cannot be eradicated.

The more comprehensive a value-system is, and the greater its value-goal, the more likely an attack on this goal becomes a *crimen laesae maiestatis* (an offense against the crown), the crime of lèse-majesté. But since such an offense has no immediate victim— for the dignity of God or the crown cannot be impaired by any such offense — such quantitative thinking does not sufficiently explain the peculiar gravity of an offense against the crown, which approaches that of radical evil. The seriousness of such an offense is only made clear by the fact that the more extensive value-system has increasing difficulty identifying an oppositional system in reality that could compete in scope and power with itself, the injured system; to identify, in other words, a system with the ability to take action against the original system and to injure it. Here the oppositional system must be accorded literally satanic power, a power that automatically raises it to the level of being the vent of evil itself.

A total value-system like religion, which in essence strives to encom-
pass the totality of the world along with all its values and value-systems,
feels itself called completely into question by the existence of Evil; the
absolute quality, the absolute, world-inclusive nature of religion permits
no neighboring or opposing systems into which evil could be displaced. Even for Manichaeism, which saw the world as resulting from
the conflict between principles of good and evil, the theological antin-
omy "How is sin possible in God's world?" is inescapable. And since
under no circumstances can sin and evil belong to one's "own" system
but only to an alien system, the question broadens to "How is the presence of an oppositional system within one's 'own' system possible?"

The resolution of this paradox is found in the nature of the ethical
demand itself. When Luther says, "Good and pious works do not make
a good and pious man, but rather a good and pious man does good and
pious works," he expresses the essence of the matter. Luther denounces
the perverting of an infinite ethical demand into a finite moral code,
which is indeed a part of the value-system but must not be confused
with it. In other words, within every value-system there exists another
completely identical system, which trait for trait completely matches
with the original and yet is its opposite, for it lacks its view toward an
infinite value-goal. It is the mask of the Antichrist, who bears Christ's
features but is Evil nonetheless.

One could speak of a specific imitation system, of an imitation in
which even the *imitatio Dei* is again imitated but where all essential elements are converted to their opposites: the infinite to the finite, the irrational to the rational, and vice-versa. And no matter how significant it is
that the infinite is lessened and degraded into the finite, and the finite
pathetically inflated to the infinite (for this is the essence of pathos),
more important than this reversal is the reversal of the ethical and the
esthetic, which is the distinguishing characteristic of an imitation
system, indeed, where the logic that drives it is to be found. For here
something is happening that changes the total ethical character of the

system: Its ethical demand is replaced by something for which really there is only one description, albeit a *contradictio in adjecto,* namely, the "esthetic demand."

Using the word "esthetic" in its broadest sense, whereby it applies to anything already formed, the "esthetic demand," in brief, is not oriented toward the ethical and infinite value-goal of the system but is based on already existing formations within the system. If every value-system finds its concrete esthetic realization in preformed or prealtered versions of the world — art in the multitude of existing artworks, science in the system of established scientific findings, politics or military strategy in the global political conditions currently in effect — and if every system is striving beyond the current situation toward its infinitely distant value-goal, in a continuous process of refinement, then, we have said, preexisting esthetic formations are eliminated from the system at the moment of their being formed and can only become the objects yet again of new formation. And even art, in so far as it is rational theory, develops by constantly turning away from what has been; theories of painting, for instance, such as perspective or atmospherics, are constantly improving "scientifically." The conservative tendency at work in every value-system, aiming at the preservation of previously formed esthetic values, plays a role, forming a countermovement within all this ongoing development, but this countermovement leads immediately *ad absurdum* when the real goal of the system is lost, i.e., when humanity in its quest toward value turns and directs its gaze backward. Yes, even conservatism as a value-system in itself becomes senseless, paralyzed, "reactionary," as soon as it forgets its own living goal, the preservation of the past in continuous and living development, and clings solely to preformed, rigid ideas. This is what Plotinus meant by "forgetting the divine origin of things," here we have the reversion of the preexisting and the preformed into the chaotic state of *apeiron* (the unknowable), even though they might be preserved for a time in petrified form; the man who thus perverts his value-goal has lost his goodwill; his *volitio* has become reversed to *nolitio,* even that *nolitio perfecta* which Aquinas saw as constituting evil itself; he becomes a collector of lifeless objects, and for him the past and its forms are not just symbols of the infinite goals but come suddenly to be the goal itself. And so for the believer in dogma and in Scripture — to come back to our example — the visible Church is no longer the all-encompassing symbol of God that it professes to be, but is made to be God itself: In reducing the infinite quality of God to the finite quality of the visible, faith becomes mere moralizing as it is dragged down from the sphere of the ethical and into the esthetic, and the infinite imperative of faith is degraded into an esthetic one.

But this "esthetic demand" is thus also transformed into a demand for "effect," in fact can be defined as such. So while the "effect" of faith is to be found in the grace of redemption from death, which is only granted to mankind as a logical possibility and preparedness for the soul's infinite journey, the effect of grace for the literal believer rather than the man of faith is in a sense a direct reward, having an immediate and formal connection to his earthly deeds. And it is no different in all the other value-systems: the infinite goal, in fact esthetic and irrational, which results merely as an "effect," the correct automatic side effect of ethically good action: "Wealth" for the merchant, "beauty" for artists, this entirely irrational thing, is now elevated to a rational goal, and this is what defines the true essence of an imitation system, that it is seemingly no longer distinct at all from the original value-system, but in fact stands in strict opposition to it. The imitation system is everywhere, whether it is the financial mercenaries that are built into the system of commerce, or the snobbism that characterizes a feudal society, or the imitation system of kitsch within the value-system of art: All these are, although in miniature, images of the system of the Antichrist.

And it is the system of "reaction" in the value-system of conservatism. For the "esthetic demand" is based on the past *per se,* which transposes it into a value-goal, a "false" value-goal, and elevates it into a false value subject, to an Anti-God, the bearer of evil, whose anti-ethical demands dogmatically intervene in the living evolution of the original system and its autonomy. And precisely because this is how "esthetic demand" functions, it becomes the mission of kitsch as an esthetic phenomenon to be the representative of the ethically evil.

V. KITSCH

Kitsch and Tendentious Art

First, one objection: If the dogmatic is in fact supposed to be evil for every value-system, if art in fact should refuse to be subject to any external influences, then every kind of tendentious art would *a priori* be representing evil; indeed, it would be dubious whether the medieval subordination of art to religion had not contradicted the essential nature of art. And nonetheless medieval art survived, artworks survive today whose outspokenly tendentious nature is undeniable; Lessing's didactic writings, Gerhart Hauptmann's *The Weavers,* and Russian films all survive.

So one cannot simply insist that all tendentious art is kitsch, no matter how much the imitation system (as represented by kitsch) is suited to be subordinated to extra-artistic ends, no matter how much one feels the danger of kitsch for all tendentious art. Take Zola, whom no one would accuse of creating kitsch: Looking at his *Quatre Evangiles,* where he wanted to set down his socialist, anticlerical convictions, one sees a completely utopian situation in the frame of a naturalistic novel, a condition that would certainly never have come about even after the arrival of a classless society, a condition in which good and evil are judged not by future moral concepts but are attached to good socialists and bad anti-socialists in accordance with moral concepts valid in 1890. And even though Zola himself is far from kitsch, in this process one sees all the dangers that are provoked by the penetration of an alien system inside the autonomous realm of an art form. It is almost a textbook example of the effectiveness of the dogmatic within a value-system. For if it is part of the essence of our age that every value-system maintain its autonomy under all circumstances, if this entirely ethical behavior — and therein lies the tragedy of our age — finds expression in an all-out war among values, then the rape of one value-system by another is, to put it anthropomorphically, like the conduct of an enemy army in occupied territory, i.e., it allows itself things that its ethics would forbid it at home. And if art — which in itself has no theme "of its own," for it is a representation, always requiring alien value-realms, drawing even its major theme, love, from the value-realms of the erotic — if art, more than any other system, is able to tolerate intrusion from without, so that today art and especially literature have become more than ever a playground for every imaginable alien value-system, if we have not only patriotic and socialist tendentious art but also novels about sport and other special interests, then all of this has a least common denominator perhaps most obvious where love poetry turns pornographic, i.e., just where the erotic value-system becomes dogmatic and literature is transformed into erotic tendentious art; the infinite goal of love reverts to the finite, its irrationality is pulled back toward the finite, the goal becomes a series of rational sex acts. And it is no different, if less crass, for Zola the utopian to shift the vital value-system of socialism (and back then it *was* still young and vital) into the time and circumstances of 1890; in drawing the infinite goal of socialism into the finite, he "finitizes" the system itself, but in so doing perverts its ethos into rationalistic moralizing. Not only does this offend the principle of a genuine utopia, which logically must be infinitely distant from reality, but, most significantly, it also transforms the artist's "good" work into the despised "beautiful"; of course, it cannot be forbidden for the artist to describe socialists, patriots, and sports and religious figures, it cannot be disallowed to describe conditions that cry out for military or pacifist solutions — in just this sense Hauptmann's *Weavers* is legitimate tendentious literature — indeed, the poet must depict them, for the world in all its aspects must remain the subject of an "expanded naturalism," but it is just this expanded naturalism and its truthfulness, which is the only criterion of an autonomous art, that may not observe these value-systems in any way other than as objects of faithful description: It must show them in their incompleteness, in their evolution, "as they really are," and not "as it would like them to be," or as they would themselves like to be, completed in the realm of the finite and made concrete in a way in which they never can be.

The Reactionary Technique of "Effect"

The essence of kitsch is the confusion of ethical and esthetic categories; kitsch wants to produce not the "good" but the "beautiful." And if this means that the kitsch novel, even while often using quite naturalistic language, i.e., the vocabulary of reality, describes the world not as it really is but as it is hoped and feared to be, and if quite analogous tendencies turn up in the fine arts as well, if kitsch in music depends exclusively on effect — one need only think of the so-called bourgeois salon music, remembering that in many respects the music industry of today is its overbred offspring — still one must concede that no art can work without some effect, without a smattering of kitsch. In the dramatic arts, kitsch becomes a structural and artistic component, and there is even an entire genre, a specifically bourgeois one, namely, opera, in which effect is the principal structuring element; and one should not forget that opera by its very nature is distinctly "historical," and that that relationship between artwork and public where the "effect" is actually revealed is a matter of the empirical, the earthbound. The means employed for effect are always "proven," and they can hardly be increased any more than the number of possible dramatic situations could be increased; that which is past and proven appears over and over again in kitsch; in other words (a stroll through any art exhibit will confirm this), kitsch is always subject to the dogmatic influence of the past — it will never take its vocabulary of reality from the world directly but will apply pre-used vocabularies, which in its hands rigidify into cliché, and here is the *nolitio,* the rejecting of goodwill, the turning away from the divine cosmic creation of values.

Kitsch-Romanticism

This reversion to the historical, which is the hallmark of kitsch, is by no means restricted to technical or formal considerations. For even though its value-system is likewise based on the fear of death, and, in line with its innate conservatism, tries to provide humanity with an existential certainty plucked from the imminent darkness, kitsch is still just reactionary, because it is an imitation system, and just as it foreshortens its view of the future, for example, and is satisfied with counterfeiting the finite reality of earthly life, so its view of the past is likewise truncated. The historical novel can be seen as the product of a quite legitimate Romanticism that clings to the values of the past and sees the continuous unfolding of history as a reflection of the eternal. But this completely legitimate and in principle unchangeable attitude of the conservative spirit is discredited the moment it is employed out of personal motivations: for example, in times of irrational and revolutionary turmoil, if it is used as an escape from the irrational, as a flight into an idyllic historic past, where fixed conventions still applied. This personal longing for a better and safer world makes more understandable the current rejuvenation of interest in the historical and in the historical novel; but, since this longed-for historical past is also "beautiful," this is a move into an area that belongs to the sphere of influence of kitsch. And in fact nowhere is this longing satisfied so simply as in kitsch; just as once the blood-and-thunder novels of knights and knaves were a response to this romantic tendency, and where even then the vocabulary of reality from the immediate historical past was replaced by prefabricated clichés, so, today, we flee from reality clearly in search of a world of fixed conventions, a kind of world of our fathers, where everything was good and right, seeking, in short, an immediate connection to the past; similarly, kitsch always technically copies its immediate predecessor, and the means it employs to do this are always astonishingly simple — one could really call this the symbolic power of kitsch — indeed, it suffices to bring some historical figure from the recent past like Emperor Franz Josef onto the operetta stage: His mere presence creates that atmosphere of reassurance that people need. And it is no different in the rose-colored world of kitsch novels.

Confusing the Finite with the Infinite

One must distinguish between annulling death and fleeing death, between shedding light on the irrational and fleeing from the irrational. Kitsch is found in flight, it is constantly fleeing into the rational. The techniques of kitsch, which are based on imitation, are rational and operate according to formulas; they remain rational even when their result has a highly irrational, even crazy, quality. For though kitsch, as an imitation system, is obliged to coincide in all its aspects with art, the artwork's methodology as such cannot be imitated — all that can be imitated are its simplest forms. It is quite significant — and nowhere is this so obvious as in poetry, but also somewhat in music — that kitsch must always revert to the most primitive methods, precisely because it completely lacks any imagination of its own: Pornography, whose reality vocabulary consists, obviously, of sex acts, is mostly a mere series of such acts; the kitsch detective novel consists of a series of identical victories over the criminal, the sentimental kitsch novel is an array of indistinguishable good deeds rewarded and bad deeds punished; incidentally, here the monotonous vocabulary units of reality are fitted into a method of primitive syntax, a constant, rhythmic drumbeat.

If such novelistic situations were translated into reality, they would be not fantastic but simply crazy, for what they lack is that meaning from a syntactic system which is the mark of an authentic work of art. The subjective and creative freedom of selecting and forming the reality vocabulary is here no longer at work within a system, and the connection between the reality base and its ultimate form is at the same time as loose and as illogical as that between a building and the stuck-on ornamentation of kitsch architecture. And probably it is this inability to copy any systematically creative work of art that leads any imitative system (and not just that of art) to justify betraying the highest value-aim of the imitated system through an appeal to dark and Dionysian forces, to the pulse of the blood, to the emotions. It is almost immaterial whether this appeal to the emotions is undertaken by a pseudoscience, a pseudophilosophy, or a pseudopolitics, or simply by a sentimental novel, for any appeal to the emotions or to the irrational will always, in kitsch, return to imitation, to rational formulaic means; for example when the kitsch novel aims at reproducing Hamsun's closeness to nature by an overdone emphasis on autochthonic themes and peasant virtues, or when it similarly incorporates Dostoievsky's infinite search for God into every second work of popular fiction, then the efforts that kitsch makes to distance itself from its own peculiar primitive methods do not conceal but actually expose quite clearly the discrepancy here, that the finite is being patheticized, that is, elevated to the level of the infinite, as is always the case when a finite and minor value appears with the claim of universal validity.

The Representation of Evil

And just this gratification of physical urges through finite and rational means, precisely this patheticizing of the finite to the infinite, this conscious working at "the Beautiful" gives kitsch that touch of mendacity behind which one senses the ethically evil. For the flight from death, which is not the annulment of death, this shaping of the world, which nonetheless leaves the world no further formed, is still just an apparent annulment of time: The goal of every value-system, the transformation of time into a simultaneous system, is likewise the goal of every imitation system, including kitsch. But since no new formative action occurs, since the irrational is not in any way clarified, merely substituting one rational definition with another, kitsch never attains the annulment of time, and its flight from death is just "killing time."

The maker of kitsch does not create inferior art, he is not an incompetent or a bungler, he cannot be evaluated by esthetic standards; rather, he is ethically depraved, a criminal willing radical evil. And since it is radical evil that is manifest here, evil *per se,* forming the absolute negative pole of every value-system, kitsch will always be evil, not just kitsch in art, but kitsch in every value-system that is not an imitation system; for whoever works for the effect of beauty, whoever seeks only that affective gratification that makes one gasp, "beautiful!", that is, the radical esthete, will use any and all means without hesitation to achieve this effect of beauty: The gigantic work of kitsch that Nero himself arranged with the fireworks display of burning Christians in his gardens, while playing the lute — not for nothing were Nero's greatest ambitions theatrical.

Every era of disintegration of values was also an era of kitsch. The disintegrating classical culture of Imperial Rome created kitsch, and the present era, standing at the end of that process which the medieval worldview began, must once again find its representation in the esthetically evil. For times of final loss of values are grounded on evil and the fear of evil, and the art that is to be their most obvious expression must also be an expression of the evil at work within them.

A New Synthesis of Value-Systems

Of course if the thesis is correct that the world's historical legacy to succeeding generations and to eternity is solely the ethically worthy act, including its equivalent esthetic result, then kitsch has never been the expression of the lifestyle of an age. For then the kitsch created through all these millennia just disappeared, and nothing survived except genuine art. Or did a lot of kitsch just change its signature? Do we not take much art to be full, legitimate, expressive of its time, which in fact once was manufactured art, and conventional kitsch? One must be extremely cautious dealing with assessments of historical phenomena, being mindful of constantly changing patterns of appreciation; it would be difficult to determine a hierarchy of Egyptian art today, and in the last analysis it is probably not possible to say what is just epigonal provincial art of Fayum or Pompeii, preserved only by accident, and what should be accounted as the true expression of the age and its style. Certainly the parallels between the final days of the ancient world and the present time are significant — but can they be extended unproblematically to the field of art?

And yet this objection — if it can be justified at all — is weak. For it does not much matter if what is clearly seen as kitsch today, if what is despised and taken as the representation of evil today, if this oddly undervalued and yet so profitable phenomenon will still be existing in a number of years or whether it will then be judged differently. History is not quite absolute immortality, and even if kitsch is ephemeral, if its manifestations already are slipping into oblivion, even there providing us with a proof of our thesis, and even though the ethical act and its esthetically valid result will easily outlive today's kitsch, nonetheless for them, too, the era of darkness and of complete oblivion will also break: History is a function of viewpoint and distance, and its only absolutes are method and idea. And if it is an expression of our age that the fearful tension between its good and its evil shows in its art as well, this may fade with the passing of time, its contours may blur, but it will remain timeless like every correct view (provided its method is correct) and will remain valid for all ages and allows one to conclude that in every era that had to live and suffer under similar conditions, even in the late Roman empire, things were just the same, regardless of whether their forms of kitsch have survived until now, regardless of whether they are viewed now as kitsch or as art. But one inheritance we have from the late ancient world, from the horrors of religious strife that it struggled through, an inheritance that has become both historical and spiritual actuality, is the merging of value-systems, which then were as strife-torn as today, into an organon of a new religion and a new religiosity, which will be the fruit of a present whose deepest need is the search for faith.

And that is what matters. Not until a higher value-system has absorbed and conciliated the warring of autonomous individual value-systems, not until these individual systems have again become subservient to an overriding Platonic Idea, have been fitted into its hierarchy, only then will the tension and convulsive struggles between different groups disappear, not just from the world, but from the soul of man, whose discord is identical with the world's discord of values. The counter-reaction to the presence of evil in every individual gives rise to the world's question: "What should we do?"; the esthetic reverts back to the ethical, so that unity may be restored to the world; for even though one day it may again sink into disintegration, for as long as it exists, this unity will exclude non-art and will be visibly embodied as such in the existence of beauty.

The Spirit
in an
Unspiritual Age (1934) [1]

translated by John Hargraves

HUMANITY today has been overtaken by a peculiar contempt for words, a contempt that is almost revulsion. The easy confidence that people could persuade one another by means of words and language has been radically lost; *parlare* has taken on a negative sense, and parliaments are being undone by their own aversion to the activity of parleying. Anywhere a conference is called, it meets subject to the scorn and skepticism of pundits who all too generally agree on the impossibility of agreement. Each one knows that the other speaks a different language, inhabits a different value-system, that every country is imprisoned inside its own value-system. Not just every country, but every vocation: The merchant cannot persuade the soldier, nor the soldier the merchant, and they understand each other only to the extent that each concedes the other's right to use whatever means he has at his disposal, to employ

[1.] Hermann Broch, "Geist und Zeitgeist," *Schriften zur Literatur 2: Theorie* (Frankfurt am Main: Suhrkamp, 1975), pp. 177–218.

his own values ruthlessly, to break any treaty should he choose to invade and conquer his enemy. Whether one calls it cynicism or not, never before, at least not in Western European history, has the world so candidly and openly admitted that words mean nothing and, moreover, that any attempt at mutual understanding and agreement is not even worth the effort. Never before has it been resigned so openly to thinking that the only means it could, or should, use, is power, the power of strong over weak.

This is not to bewail the fact that the world is the way it is, nor to blame mankind for this state of affairs. For mankind, the situation is desperate, for having lost faith in words, it despairs of the spirit, too, the spirit of its own humanity, that spirit which works through language. The word is nothing without the spirit, which can live nowhere else but in the word; whoever kills the spirit, kills the word, and whoever desecrates the word, desecrates the spirit; the two are bound inseparably. Over and over again, humanity loses its language, and over and over again the spirit, the absolute, slips from its grasp, time and again humanity is thrown back to the muteness of its dim origins, still apparent today in the apathy of primitive peoples; it is thrown back to their violence, their obscure suffering. And it is truly suffering, for mankind will never lose its aspirations to godliness, and no matter how depraved, no matter how far fallen from the spirit, it will keep on striving toward the spirit. This mute silence weighs heavily on a world that has lost language and spirit, for it has had to put its faith in power, and in murder, without which there is no power. Muteness now rules both individuals and groups, and it is the muteness of murder.

Yet despite this muteness, the world is full of voices. Not the voices of dialogue and discourse, but muddled voices, as if from a broken loudspeaker, each shouting down and drowning out the others, a Babel of languages and ideas ignoring each other. Amidst all this, the Church broadcasts its message, but mechanically, unceremoniously, drowned out, banalized and annihilated by the clamor of earthly life. It is the awful wordless clamor that goes with murder — rhetorical in itself, a muteness elevated to the noise and pathos of the rhetorical. It is a muteness that sounds like speech, but is not — a syntax of shouting, an element of language, admittedly, of just its wordless part, but in this wordlessness there is only fear, or desperation, or courage, about to erupt. The rhetorical knows no dialogue, no argument or counterargument, it comes not from the sphere of the intellect, but from darkness. It does not convince, but enthralls and fascinates through the power of darkness, through the allure of darkness, through this danger that no one can escape, for there is no one in whom this same darkness does not dwell, no one safe from this danger beyond logic, even madness. Wherever this dark silence finds an outlet, exploding into life, it goes for the heart: It can elevate, crush, or open the heart, moving it to raptures of lunacy, ecstasy, passion — or destruction and murder. Rhetoric, that anthem of both heroism and desperation, serves the religion of power.

But with such sincerity! Muteness cannot lie, only words can lie — how honest, then, to admit the dishonesty of words, to know that it is the spirit and only the spirit that lets itself be put to such infamous use, what courage, to commend the lie to the service of power! It is an honesty, an attitude that originated with Machiavelli, even though it appears in what we call "Americanism" to have found its latest commercial and unpolished form. Nonetheless, the world has always been honest — it believed just as honestly in God as in witches, it believed with all honesty in the spirit. From this viewpoint, honesty is no virtue, but simply a general human trait, the irresistible human impulse to believe in anything that seems logical or plausible, or likely to satisfy the needs of instinct. So for the brutal man, the man who cares only, as the saying goes, for "brute facts" (facts both brute and mute) — is his honesty different from other kinds of honesty? Does it have a specific criterion?

Indeed it does, and it may be found in a certain point of view that has developed since the Renaissance, a viewpoint that can also quite rightly be ascribed to Machiavelli, and that one might call the positivist viewpoint. The West owes so much to positivism, which likely brought Europe to world dominance (Columbus would not have reached America, nor would the steam engine have been discovered, if Europe had not cared about the "brute facts") — so it may seem blasphemous to blame positivism for the mute (and brute) gangster methods with which Europe is now betraying and destroying its own achievements. What does the practical man's basis of "facts," the brutally ruthless man, the man of instinctive self-interest (a trait he likes to call Americanism), what does this man have to do with the man of intellect, with the man of science, a man whom he despises? What does positivist intellectuality have to do with the atmosphere of murder now weighing on the world? With the silence of murder? And yet they are related, for gangsters, merchants, soldiers, and scientists, all are the children of one age.

Science's responsibility is a metaphysical one; it has no "guilt"; on the contrary, its guilt is its purity, that purity of being based on "the facts," which science must be, by its own infallible logic. Ever since science was freed from the bonds of scholasticism it has distanced itself more and more from speculation. How slowly this has gone can be seen from the speculative humbug still governing medicine in the eighteenth century; only now is it beginning to approach its methodological ideal, that is, to accept as scientifically "real" reality only what can be verified by sight, sound, touch, or instruments of magnification like telescopes. For this "real" reality, not even mathematical calculations suffice, since the purely mathematical revelation of truth required finding an unimpeachable way of applying mathematics to itself (which it did in Brouwer-Weyl intuitionism). But the exclusion of everything speculative from science meant the beginning of the exclusion of language. Certainly there are sciences that live from and in language, such as history, and the whole array of natural science disciplines: Neither medicine nor botany could exist without linguistic commentary; even the disciplines furthest removed from language, mathematics and logic, could not function without an introduction or procedural rules, which are given in "natural" language. But we note that language here has another function than it does in conceptual or dialectic speculation. For example, if all the events of history had been filmed continuously, we could have spared ourselves a good part of written history, and one day our weekly newsreels may actually be used for this purpose. The use of precise, mechanically objective presentation methods is growing in all fields of knowledge, from replicating historical documents to audio and visual recordings of biological and natural processes; the overall aim is to exclude as much as possible the "interpreting" individual and his unreliable personal language, and thus reach that ideal of pure description and representation that Kirchoff demanded of physics and Ranke, on the same principle, demanded of history, that is, "simply to describe how it was." And to a certain extent, the near-complete autonomy of mathematical expression in the natural sciences is a response to this demand for an objective representation based mutely on facts, independent of anything human. For mathematics is largely dissociated from the mathematician, he cannot interpret it subjectively; either it offers a picture of the facts — the parabola as the depiction of a free trajectory — or it does not: It is precise, mute, a language without a subject.

Of course the mission of mathematics is not exhausted in linguistic representation. When Kant says a field of knowledge is a science only to the extent that it includes mathematics — the whole philosophic orthodoxy of his time (and apostasy from it) is contained in these words — he surely meant mathematical representation, but something else as well: provability. The immense, balanced construct of mathematics is based on tautology, and because mathematics itself is built on logic, it includes every conceivable logical structure that could exist between things, or more correctly, every new discovery in mathematics expands its range but defines a new possible logical structure for the real world as well. Thus, on the one hand, mathematics gives us a more detailed, complex, and extensive likeness of all universal logical structures, and is thus *a priori* their "linguistic" expression, while on the other hand it goes beyond replication, since it is now part of the world, and becomes, in both a Kantian and also a metaphysical sense, a "condition of possible experience of the world,"[2] an experience that begins with the countability of things. It is the connection of this curious metaphysical quality (i.e., being a "condition of possible experience") to the tautological character of mathematics, applying what is *a priori* correct (because it is a tautology) to the things of this world — it is this link that gives mathematics its peculiar reliability, its value as proof, and the exclusivity of its proof value, an exclusivity that can be seen as the basis of Kant's statement. For the essence of science is proof and provability.

So this is the honesty of positivism: Acknowledge no reality that cannot be perceived by the senses or supported by mathematical proof. It may have little connection with the honesty of common life — whose main sense organ is the stomach, and whose mathematics is that of money — but the reason for the common rejection of any kind of spirit or any connection with the spiritual is evident from this viewpoint. For the spirit has surrendered, has had to surrender. There can be nothing spiritual that doubts the spirit, that does not believe in the Logos, which is the mouthpiece of the spirit, its vessel and its form, nothing that does not strive for that absolute which is based on spirit and the Logos. This was the position of classical Platonism, and also of Christian Platonism. And within such belief in the Logos, whether known as the Word of God or something else, every linguistically logical deduction has that same provability, an ideal of all science, which today only mathematics can claim. Positivist honesty is the honesty of the doubting Thomas, doubting in the true sense of the word, even if, like Thomas, it does not deny a reality that extends beyond the palpable and demonstrable — it has simply lost hold of this reality, with no means of finding it again. A way of thinking that stands outside of belief must strive for the perceivable *[zum Wahrnehmbaren streben]* instead of for the truth, and instead

2. Kant's *Bedingung möglicher Erfahrung*, from the *Critique of Pure Reason*.

of striving to know that which really moves the world *[zum Wirkenden]*, it must strive for a reality whose existence it knows only insofar as it is mathematically replicable; it is radically anti-philosophical, or, what amounts to the same thing here, radically anti-theological. It shares rational method with philosophy and theology, but since it excludes philosophy's two basic premises, the Logos and the Spirit, it is forced to relegate every true philosophical problem — and it is already doing this today — to the realm of the mystical, a realm that real philosophy will not tolerate but that theology considers almost heresy, because both philosophy and theology strive for a rational understanding of the world in its totality.

With unique sensitivity, the Catholic Church has discerned the dangers of the rising spirit of positivism. Her rejection, for example, of the unmediated introspectiveness of mysticism attests to this sensitivity, but it is even more marked in her concern with natural sciences: for in itself it is of no importance to the Church whether the sun goes round the earth or the earth round the sun, because from her standpoint a third or fourth astronomical solution would be   just as possible: What the Church takes issue with, and must constantly battle, is the anti-philosophical, positivist intellectual stance, which deprives life of its central viewpoint — whether it be called God or the Logos, in this case, God — and replaces it with an infinite number of viewpoints. What the Church did often seemed suicidal, for she fought against the intellect, which forged the Church's weapons against external foes, and even worked with these weapons for the expansion of the Holy Faith. From this viewpoint it might seem a good thing to some that the Church almost always yielded to the new intellectualism in the end, but that cannot be decided here, or probably anywhere. It is certain that the Church survives intact, even if "real" life is no longer played out inside, but outside her walls (symbol of the Vatican island in metropolitan Rome!), and it is certain that what is occurring outside those walls is precisely what she wished to prevent, the rule of the positivist spirit, the struggle under its aegis of "all against all," and the extinguishing of everything that could truly be called spiritual, that is, that spirit which seeks truth, rather than the perceivable.

To philosophy's credit, it must be said that it has always resisted secularization. This may sound strange, since no one has ever tried to impose secularization upon philosophy, except for the hypothetical *Zeitgeist* — the spirit of the age. But, far from being so hypothetical after all, this *Zeitgeist* was the logical component of intellectual evolution, and it was in particular a logical crisis within scholasticism that inevitably led to new forms and new extra-scholastic modes of verification. Secular science was there in any case, and philosophy had to come to terms with it, if it were not to lose its own claim to being scientific. But none of the great philosophers who had appeared since that time had forgotten that philosophy's real task was theology, and all their aspirations were theological. This was true of Descartes, of Spinoza, of Leibniz, of Kant (German Idealism can really be seen as an attempt to create a Protestant-scholastic universal *organon),* true of Kierkegaard, and notably — as if finally religion had to return to its origins — true of Hermann Cohen's faithfully staunch Neo-Kantianism, and of Edmund Husserl.

Certainly none of these philosophies were untinged by positivist influences, not even Plato, not to mention Aristotle, and since no intellectually vital phenomenon can free itself from the *Zeitgeist* (nor should it, if it wishes to survive), the influence of positivist elements has grown more and more significant; this is especially demonstrable with German Idealism. But it would be totally wrong to grant positivist thought the status of philosophy; again: No philosophy is possible without the Platonic-divine primal experience of the individual Self in isolation. So the emergence of an actual "positivist philosophy" can be blamed not on philosophy or philosophers but rather on that curious breed, the "experts"; among philosophers, these are the "officials." What arose here was that singular absurdity, "empirical philosophy," which broke up the unitary body of philosophy into many viewpoints, in true positivist fashion, resulting in the amazing phenomenon of a philosophy of history, of law, of race, of technology, ornamental gardening, stamp collecting, or theater directing. Mostly they consist of a hodgepodge of special theories and so-called thoughts the specialist has about his area of expertise, of which the former can occasionally be very interesting — for instance, the countless inductive hypotheses about the laws of history — while the so-called thoughts have precious little to do with thinking, at least philosophical thinking. All this nonsense, actually just misunderstanding, began within those enlightened circles of laymen in the eighteenth century who were filled with ignorance and contempt for everything theological, and thus everything philosophical, and took everything that looked like theory to be philosophy. This then gave rise to Voltaire's *Philosophie de l'histoire,* Lamarck's *Philosophie de la Nature,* [3] which contained the first theories of evolution, and the crowning achievement of this whole process, totally in line with these specialized philosophies, or rather, nonphilosophies, was the true "positivism" of Comte, which in its non-philosophical part was a new historical science and theory: sociology.

The extent to which philosophy has become contaminated can be seen in these "empirical philosophies." Moreover, such a positivistically tainted philosophy becomes the nearest thing to rhetoric, and the danger of this happening seems practically inevitable with a philosophy whose focus lies neither within itself nor in God, because it is then subject to every external dictate. There are hundreds of examples of such rhetorical philosophies: German philosophy in particular has provided quite remarkable examples of this, and not only by a damnable misuse of philosophical jargon, as seen in the various philosophies of war, for example, but also in one of its finest variants, the thought of Nietzsche (that most untheological, antitheological of thinkers!). The alternation of the positivistic viewpoint between "life" and "spirit" is perhaps most visible here, in the rhetorical, even where it is elegant and almost poetic;

3. Broch may have been referring to Lamarck's *L'Histoire naturelle des animaux sans vertèbres.* — Trans.

in the rhetorical, we no longer have the search for an irrefutable truth through language, grounded in Logos, the word — nor do we have logical persuasion, conviction, or divine *ratio*. We find, rather, something ultimately based in the irrational, something that can turn at any moment into madness, into ecstatic rapture, into the most high-minded delusion, as with Nietzsche, but also into the mad depravity that derives from the vile rhetoric of the mob.

And so positivism's only truly philosophical accomplishment may be that after four hundred years it has abandoned all its quasi-philosophical aspirations and come to recognize honesty as its true scientific duty. It has relegated all philosophical topics to the realm of mysticism (even the age of Comte was overshadowed by mysticism or, worse, occultism), limited its activity, and confined itself to its own scientific core, which today is quite clearly defined: a strict, methodical critique based on mathematics and logic, which belongs to the realm of "muteness." And even this work cannot be done without the Logos and the Spirit, but in the view of radical (and philosophical) positivism, these two terms also belong to mysticism, and it will have nothing to do with them; for the positivist they are neither apprehensible by the senses nor supportable by mathematics. At best, they belong to those unknowable preconditions of life that cannot be probed by science.

The unknowable preconditions of life: with unmatchable authority, the following words stand at the beginning of history, holding within them, as if clenched in a fist, the germ and the growth of all history: "In the beginning was the Word . . . and the Spirit of God moved upon the face of the waters." [4] And more powerful still than knowing that all historical progress is inevitably yoked to word and to spirit, to law and to destiny, greater even than this prophetic knowledge is the awareness of the mysterious dual origin of the human soul contained in that opening statement. For nothing can ever be said about history that does not issue from knowledge of the human soul, for it is primarily the soul that both reflects and is reflected by history. The statement that that great author,

[4.] Broch conflates two quotations: resp., *John I*, 1 and *Genesis I*, 2.

his hand guided by God himself, hurled back at his Creator, like an accusation, seeing the elemental duality of a God who conceals his origin while revealing two concurrent creative principles, as though he himself were subject to them — this accusation makes the goal of all human actions the rediscovery of a lost divine harmony. This accusation, the most passionate indictment any creature can make of its creator, is born of a deep and fearful insight into the heart and the unchangeable nature of man. This first sentence has been varied and interpreted thousands of times, and will be as often as mankind, in fear and trembling, becomes aware of its own existence and its consciousness, as often as it is struck by the question of its ultimate conditionality, as was Descartes with his *Cogito ergo sum,* which was just one variation. But even if this first sentence had never been written down, adapted, or interpreted — if all of this had never happened, if it had never clearly and consciously been put into words, even then it would be impossible for anyone, even the most naïve (or perhaps especially the naïve), not to feel and to know intuitively the dual origin of the human soul. And so every human being would feel that mysterious call, that mystical impulse to close this gap, and not be forced to choose between the primacy of Spirit or Logos. And this is only the first stage; beyond this is the need to strive for a unity in which lies the fulfillment of human destiny, the fulfillment of history.

One must not object that such mystical optimism requires religious belief. Still less can one say it legitimates *sub rosa* a taboo historical philosophy, one of Augustinian stamp at that (where Logos and Spirit come from God). Honorable objections perhaps, but not applicable or justified in this case. We remove religious belief from this entire discussion, even though the power of that first scriptural passage ["In the beginning was the Word"] alone is mystically awe-inspiring. The discussion here is not of religion or the religious viewpoint, though the time is not far off when people will want to hear and speak of nothing else. No, here and in what follows, religious belief is not required, but at most just that self-evident *religio* without which there is no desire for knowledge, not even the knowledge of atheism. Though historical philosophy is rather popular nowadays — even Augustine owes his current popularity to the misapprehension that he is a historical philosopher — we need say no more about it. It already goes practically without saying that we reject so-called historical philosophical constructs, almost all of which attempt to prove various theses, theories, hypotheses, and prophecies in the course of history (and interpret it accordingly): Even the great name of Hegel could not legitimate such a process, nor that of the Hegelian Marx, far less, then, their ridiculous successors Biedermann, Jentzsch,[5] etc., or the attempts of Panslavist dabblers to manufacture a history based on Slav racial supremacy. (All of this is reminiscent of the Britons' "scientifically" provable descent from the Hebrews.) And so all attempts to show that the prophecies of this first statement are concretely and historically accurate would have the same flaw. For no matter how clear it is that human history is yoked to both Word and Spirit, or their external forms, law and destiny, no matter that the battle of these two principles for control of mankind's soul is the force that drives history, still, the unity of observable history should not be appropriated or explained by any given philosophical system: that is a matter for parlor pseudo-philosophers. No, the oneness of observable history lets us learn what man is, what Spirit is, what the Logos is. This is no longer historical philosophy, but genuine philosophy, or rather the subject matter of philosophy (which one might call existentialism).

If we wanted even to use dialectic methods and show that the conflict of two principles results in a disjunction, producing four possible logical solutions (entailing a large and complex expansion of Hegelian dialectic), then the four solutions would look like this:

1. Victory of the one principle (here, primacy of Spirit)
2. Shared victory of both principles (here, unity of Logos and Spirit)
3. Victory of the other principle (here, primacy of Logos)

[5.] Gustav Biedermann (1815–1883), Austro-Czech philosophical writer, and Karl Jentsch (1833–1917), German journalist. Their respective works, *Philosophie als Begriffswissenschaft* (1915) and *Geschichts philosophische Gedanken* (1903) were part of Broch's personal library.

4. Defeat of both principles, i.e., the whole conflict and the problem itself become pointless (here, invalidation of both Logos and Spirit)

Here the phases of the conflict, how and when they occur in history, are not significant; it would be a simple seminar exercise to see whether this gives new support to Hegel's reversal theory. It may not even matter that such clumsy logic schemes demonstrate once again the inevitability of periodic disintegration of values. The only significant fact here, which we knew even without constructing a dialectical disjunction, is that there have been two moments in known European intellectual history when a unity of Logos and Spirit seemed attained or attainable. These two moments were the classical Golden Age and the High Middle Ages. Moreover, it remained for the current age to make the fourth case of the disjunction concrete, that is, the eradication of both Spirit and Logos (now meaningless) from its life, although not from its rhetoric. (This was formally appropriate, since one of the great contributions of modern logic has been the discovery of the meaninglessness of certain questions whose validity had previously been beyond question.) It might be even more significant to note the distance, the "vertical drop" separating mankind's current psychic state from one that approaches its highest ideals, a gulf so tremendous that one can appreciate the Church's view, which claims to see here in appalling clarity the abyss between good and evil, between Christ and Antichrist.

Has man today truly renounced Spirit and the Logos? At least outwardly, the general world situation would certainly indicate this; the world's descent into the muteness of positivism, the rigorousness of the scientific consciousness which consigns the terms *Spirit* and *Logos* to the domain of mysticism: All this looks like renunciation. But to renounce something does not mean one is free of it, and it is probably more than just mystical optimism to believe that a prophecy that has proved true for tens of thousands of years will prove true for hundreds of thousands as well. And aside from this, there is still the conviction that the nature of humanity is historical, and this belief is not limited (as with Dilthey,[6] say) to understanding the structure of human spirit from its history, but goes beyond this to a belief in the unchangeability of humanity, in a permanence that approaches the divine nature of the Logos. And this belief is outside of and beyond history; it has the axiomatic certainty of the inner experience of life, it is the Platonic experience as such. One has to accept that what history and historical evolution teach us could all be undone in an instant of worldwide catastrophe, if not in one hundred thousand, then possibly in two hundred thousand years. So it is empty talk, *a priori,* no matter what dialectic or logic one uses, to advance claims for a stability in world history (and thus human history) that is more or less dictated by historical necessity, or to show that even in its denial the Logos has its hand in the game. (Moreover, this could later prove to be an error of the historical observer.) Truly, this would all be pointless and meaningless were it not for the help of Platonic experience. If it were not for this, if the Platonic experience were not a constant presence in life, if people were really constituted the way vulgar materialism imagines them to be, then no one in this world, particularly this positivistically oriented world, would ever have had the idea that there could exist another realm beyond the rational one of the visible and provable, a completely unfathomable and unknowable world. Certainly this realm of the unknowable was not set up especially to include the concepts of Spirit and Logos: Positivism defines for itself the limits of its own knowledge, the scope of what it can know, and simply locates what is unattainable to it as lying outside of

6. Wilhelm Dilthey (1833–1911), German philosopher. Dilthey originated the term *Geisteswissenschaften,* or spiritual sciences, to include all the humanities and social sciences (art, literature, history, philosophy, law, sociology, religion, psychology, politics, and economics), as against the natural sciences, *Naturwissenschaften.* Dilthey believed that historical consciousness, man's consciousness of the historical relativity of all ideas, attitudes, and institutions, liberates man from absolute principles, but imposes on him the necessity of understanding all of human history. — Trans.

these limits. The fact that positivism takes the trouble to propose a realm external to itself that it calls "mystic," that it knows how small the circle is which is available to rational thought, a small enclave in the infinite variety of real life (not just physiological life, but the life of the mind as well), is significant. For in so doing, positivism's honesty, scientific in the best sense, modest and scrupulous, thereby allows the existence of and points to the so-called mystical category. Thus it acknowledges the philosophical experience, exposing the roots of all thought and perception in the eternal ground of Platonism, even though for now it is forbidden ground. Even in their negation, the Spirit and the Logos are still at work.

But it is in just this, in being barred from the Platonic, that the tragedy of our age lies, this age that has been deprived of the joy and the comfort of Platonic *ratio,* and been left instead with an ill-omened, sinister rhetoric. The tragedy of our age? Or the tragedy of philosophy? Or, more correctly, of the philosophers? None of these, in fact. Tragedy is a personal fate, and if a newspaper poll were taken to find out who felt the loss of this Platonic grounding as a personal tragedy, no one would feel this way, not even philosophers. For the world has more urgent needs, truly more tragic concerns, and the deep, yet indirect connection of these concerns with the loss of our Platonic orientation cannot be the subject of tragedy. And our philosophers are quite content to do their purely scientific work inside critically logical bounds.

And yet, that special tragic quality remains. It is simply the tragedy of man as creator, obliged to shape the world in its totality, so this totality can give him the answer to the one question that matters in his striving for unity: "How do I relate to the world and to that which I call my life?" It is the ethical question, and it is the one and only concern of all tragedy. Philosophy tried to answer this question, when it was still an intact theological entity, thus still in possession of language, its own language. All the great philosophers and the systems they built were also attempts to answer this question, so that their knowledge of the world's totality would become a self-knowledge, and thus self-evident (a fading shimmer of this hangs over the late work of Edmund Husserl). For it is not the intention of the philosopher, and never can be, to make statements about the empirically knowable world, which has no similarity to his world beyond its concrete totality. The philosopher's insight into the structure of the world is, rather, that of inner experience and insight into the nature of man, which is *per se* the "condition of all possible experience." This can be such a major and truly creative insight, just like those words of Scripture, that it can become the timeless prophecy of all that has happened and will happen in the world. But that Scripture also shows that there is no insight into human nature that is not also primarily ethical; thus, within the bounds of philosophical inquiry (which doesn't preclude the equal importance of empirical inquiry), it is the task of the philosophical human to answer not so much the question "What is the nature of the world?" as the question how one is to conduct oneself in it: not so much the question of existing as the question of doing: in short, the ethical question.

So the tragic quality starts here, but it transcends the tragedy of man the knower and creator and becomes the tragedy of the world, which, lacking an ethical system, is in disintegration. For ethics cannot live without language; in times of silence, of muteness, there has always been only the dumb show of mute ethical example, the great tragedy of blood testimony, of conviction by deed, not word, of enduring or permitting injustice, of nonresistance. And today there are certainly plenty of examples of that. Of course, one could object that it is philosophy's own fault that it has not asserted its linguistic expressiveness at a time of such great ethical need; but one could raise the same objection (and just as invalidly) at all the great thinkers of the last four hundred years, because they were not able to stop the de-theologizing of philosophy by positivism, this irresistible process whose last phases we are witnessing today. To be sure, the philosopher tries repeatedly to get back to language, and he tries all the more intensely, the more fanatical he is about the ethical nature of his task. And this starts a kind of linguistic over-compensation, which began with Nietzsche — who sensed the coming of so many dangers — but which could also be found in Kierkegaard perhaps, and is clearly apparent today in Heidegger or Karl Kraus, though in different form. It is an effort to make language itself into an Absolute, to elevate language, at least partly, into the basis of knowledge, that is, to abstract from its peculiar structure, which contains the residual of tens of thousands of years of knowledge, an insight into existence itself. And though its aim be positivist (that same positivist rationality that distinguished Nietzsche) — positivist, or rather pre-positivist, since it both absolutizes and deifies an empirical creation, language — positivist, since it creates a vague analogy between the functions of language and mathematics, which in fact has its own automatic kind of existence within the tautological — no matter how positivist this effort is, it still exhibits that mystical tendency peculiar to all forms of positivism: the mystique of language. This is rhetoric in its noblest form, a last effort to escape from silence, to overcome the ethical tragedy of muteness. If the current epoch no longer has a value center firmly anchored on a theologically based philosophy and ethics, and which could raise language to the level of reliable, binding communication, then language itself must become the mystic value center. This is not the mysticism meant by logical positivism, or "high positivism" if one can call it that, for this high positivism can only mean the equally radical mysticism of its own radically mute mathematics, and this last mystical experience refuses all expression, for it too is mute. The philosophical mysticism of language is something else, it stands at the edge of poetry — as the example of Nietzsche shows — and holds itself back from the final radicality, in the hope that poetic insight will take over the task of philosophic insight, and that its "moderated" mysticism will finally cancel out the tragedy of ethical silence.

At the center of every culture is its theology. But at its beginning is its poetry; thus Homer stood at the cradle of Greek civilization, creator of its language, builder of its myths, poet and philosopher. And in his hand he held the seed of the future.

This is the hope. Of course, to understand this hope one must agree on the meaning of the word "myth." It is not enough merely to know that myth is the primal poetic form in which the hunter and warrior peoples framed their whole cosmogony, their metaphysics, and all their knowledge of men and of nature. The order in which things happen does not explain everything. If something cannot be understood on a primal level of human existence, it cannot be understood at all. And if perhaps — and only perhaps — humankind first had to settle down to tend its flocks before its soul could begin to find lyric expression, before it could start to order its metaphysical ideas into even a primitive epistemology, nonetheless, in a higher sense everything happens simultaneously, for all that is human is timeless. And even though myth surpasses all lyric poetry in power and metaphysical impact, be it even a poem of Friedrich Hölderlin, still man can learn nothing that he does not find already formed within himself by his creator. For the common root of all philosophy, all ethical volition, all learning, but also of all literature, is knowledge of the human soul. This is the lyric content of all poetry, and what makes it poetry. But it is also perhaps the lyric content of all philosophy, which first takes shape within the self in isolation. And certainly it is the lyric content of all art, art's Platonic primal experience, its divine source. And this logical primacy of the lyrical over the mythical (even if it came afterwards), given its mission of expressing the deepest, last stirrings of human experience, in all their simplicity and divine permanence, transforms the myth into a projection of the lyric into the external world. For myth, too, concerns the simplest, deepest stirrings of the human soul, no longer in the form of a lyrical confession, but seemingly "objectively," in an external event, in the particular behavior of a concrete, visible human being, released from the level of the private, confessional lyric, calling for epic or dramatic realization. If this is so, if the human behavior or event surrounding it is of such lyric simplicity and naturalness, if it truly reveals the ultimate architecture of the human, if, in a word, it is final knowledge of the human soul, then such objectification of the lyric can be termed myth. This is the relationship of prayer to the lives of the saints; and there, too, prayer is the residual of the mystical and magical. But just as human nature is embedded in the natural world and its land-scape, cradled eternally within it, and just as its lyric song, springing from deep within itself, always sings of nature, so too the event that shapes the myth is an event from the primal depths of the heart, but an event in nature as well, a natural event, whose own metaphysical power can become so great in this function, so truly "mythic," that its lyrical source is often completely obscured by it, as if it were something small, personal, and subjective. This no longer has anything to do with hunters and shepherds, or human types (even if one wanted to trace the meta-physical extrovert to the hunter, the philosophical-lyric introvert type to the shepherd): for the mythic as well as the lyric is found in every human soul, immutable, immortal, godlike as the soul itself, and is supported by a claim to eternity that is as great as the timelessness of nature and the human soul itself. It is the great allegory of Logos and Spirit in nature, of which man is also a part, it is poetic insight *per se,* it is the eternal hope that always blooms at the bounds of rational knowledge, the hope of rediscovering a lost language in myth.

But it is just this claim on eternity that now makes this problem of myth an internal and timely question for literature. Literature would not be a part of its epoch if it did not have the same tendencies as the epoch, and reflect them; its particular themes are unimportant, although, not coincidentally, they have something to do with literature's claim on eter-nity. For it is just as obvious that the circle of relative nihilism, which is the mark of positivism, and leads it toward mysticism, must appear in every other value-field, and thus in literature as well. It appears here, for example, in the changing priority of issues. What has become of Strind-berg's issues, or Wedekind's? Yet once these were matters of near-absolute relevance. What do marriage issues matter these days? Who cares nowadays about the treatment of sexual, social, and other private matters in literature? No one wants to hear it anymore! If one remembers that all artistic creativity depends on a timelessly lyrical and mythical source, and that even in its most trivial, homespun variants, art can only work from the vantage point of eternity, if it is not to despair of and suffocate in its own irrelevance — with this in mind, one can understand the distaste and near-legitimate nausea inherent in the term "asphalt literature."[7] For what matters here is literature's claim on permanent relevance, and so, ultimately, on myth. And the more brazen, evil, violent, and incomprehensible the world becomes, the stronger this desire becomes. In the realm of the imagination, what could compete with war? What theme is great enough to stand next to it? What words can be compared with death, what phrases can provide solace enough in the deepest despair of the human heart? Only the mythology of human existence *per se,* the mythology of nature and the shape it assumes among men and gods. If there were such a mythology, not only would it secure literature and its eternal meaning, it would be a sign of faith and of a new convergence of values, that convergence necessary to put an end to the violent disintegration of values.

For the time being no such mythology exists, despite the current age's longing for it. And even though it is connected to nature and the essence of the human soul, this mythology will not be resurrected by *Blut-und-Boden* novels[8] or those of French *populisme;* such an idea is typical of positivism's lack of imagination. Neither Oedipus nor Faust

[7.] The Nazi censorship of literature blacklisted certain books that dealt with the themes of the underclass, the urban life of everyday workers, categorizing them as "asphalt literature." Broch was also critical of this type of literature if it remained at the level of social protest. — Trans.

[8.] *Blut-und-Boden* (blood and soil) literature glorified the agricultural life of the "folk." Here traditional German virtues of hard work, loyalty to family, community, and one's "folk" roots were seen as being in accord with the goals of the Nazi state. — Trans.

was a farmer. Myth cannot be created by command or even by desire. It seems there is not much variability in the creation of myth, perhaps because that basic human nature which myth expresses is of such great simplicity, and it would take major changes in the human soul before it could create a new mythic symbol, such as happened with the figure of Doctor Faust. And when a poet, impelled by that desire for myth and its eternal relevance, is driven to reformulate mythic themes, it is not just modesty that forces him to make do with what already exists; it is a process that might find a parallel in the medieval artist's constant use of variations on Biblical themes, or perhaps in the permanence of certain problems in Western philosophy, which is continually forced to make new variations of that initial scriptural statement, to reestablish continually the double origin of the world in Logos and the Spirit. Yet still we cannot speak of a new mythology, but at most of the yearning for it. Taking the two most conspicuous examples: Neither Thomas Mann's recasting of the mythic wanderer Jacob nor James Joyce's of the mythic wanderer Ulysses can be termed myth; no matter how great Mann's achievement, in heightening the traditional form of the psychological novel, he brought it right up to the border of myth, but not one step over that border; nor did Joyce, no matter how great the symbolic power with which he exploded the old novel form and created a new one. Mr. Bloom is not a mythic figure, and never will be. This is not because Joyce's attempt to destroy the old form was not totally successful, nor because in this attempt he still adhered, however virtuosically, to an old form, within the aesthetic category. It is because the character of Bloom contains all the religious nihilism and relativism of our age, and is consciously represented by him. But a mythic figure is always a figure of consolation, of religion. What happens with Thomas Mann is like calling up the last reserves, taking a position as a bridgehead to a new country, but one that does not permit us to advance into it: like the Roman bridgeheads over the Rhine and the Danube, outposts in the impenetrable land of barbaric muteness that lay before them. In contrast, Joyce's bridgehead has a postern gate, which might enable an advance into new territory: Today we cannot say if it will ever be used.

But this is all just allegory, albeit an allegory that could tell us even more. For between the muteness of radical skepticism and the muteness of radical mysticism is speech. And if this age makes myth unattainable, it is the muteness of skepticism that makes it so, the skeptical muteness of positivism, which in literature can be seen most clearly in Joyce. All of positivism's disgust with language, all its aversion to dealing with worn-out concepts, all its reluctance to deal with a tradition ossified by jargon: In Joyce all this comes to life in poetic and profoundly brilliant form. Intellectual or emotional conventions no longer apply here, everything is reduced to the most detailed explanations and (positivist!) realities. There is a premonition of this distaste, and this honesty, in Tolstoy, but how feeble, and even kindly, this seems now. Joyce treats language with exactly the same disgust, the same revulsion at the outmoded, fossilized syntax of subject and predicate, he wrings final phonetic realities out of it with just the same fury, dissects them and re-forms them into wholly new creations, totally incomprehensible to the outsider. One could almost say that here the private character of the lyric has won out again over myth, that he has retro-fitted myth back into a radical kind of lyric, so radical as to be something completely esoteric. It is at once the strongest attack on myth and the strongest rejection of it.

Should we see Joyce as paradigmatic? If so, then this would not just be "rejecting" a new mythology. This would not only rob poetry of its last hope, relegating it to the realm of superfluous art, as painting and sculpture have already been; the spirit, already incapable of expressing itself in philosophy, would now lose any hope of doing this in literature. Language, the word of God, would now finally be dead. To be sure, prophecy is a tricky business. It is not only possible that there will come a poet — a Homer of the modern age — whose role it will be to create a new mythology; a new philosopher could even be born who could make philosophy once again a theologically based universal cosmogony. This person would of course be the founder of a new religion. And with the help of such a new universally recognized philosophy, this person could put a halt to the disintegration of values, and regather all the values of the world around its central belief. All this is possible.

Let us for now assume that this state of grace will not occur, even though one day it will. What then? Have Logos and Spirit disappeared from the earth because they can no longer have a mode of expression in language? But they still do, and it is the most audible means of all, in this ever-more-silent world, and it is becoming more audible and richer all the time: It is music that, like a final sign of the Spirit and the Logos, floats above the human world in universal validity. Let us not discuss the social and economic reasons that have brought increasing incomprehension of all the other art forms; one might easily think the same is true of music, but these factors do not apply here. For man has thrown himself, in a kind of frenzy, into the arms of music, insatiably and in that radical and uncompromising manner that is a basic trait of this age, with a passion explainable only by mankind's current muteness and incomprehension, and by the deep suffering this causes. Humanity sees music as a fading shimmer of God's mercy, granted as a last hint of faith and of knowledge transcending the visible, a triumph over silence that transcends the tragic insight of rational intellect. Even in the remotest reaches he rejoices in this gift, and in listening, he becomes again what he once was, human. Music, it almost seems, is far less exposed to the dangers of this rational world than any other human activity or expression, and even the evil of separate value-systems, the inevitable *l'art pour l'art* in every work of art, seems not to have affected music: not even mechanization, which in this mechanized world one would have thought music's fate. Music has kept its smile.

However, even if music too disappeared from this world, if everything, even this last, this unmediated expression of the spirit were silenced, then all we would be left with is rational thought, which clings to what it can see in desperate earnest, aware of the limits of its knowledge, saying *"ignorabimus"* as it consigns any questions about what is beyond these limits to the mystical. Even here, in this view, this extremely logical view, the spirit is still at work, as *agens,* as a higher power that no longer belongs to the sphere of reason and which cannot be understood by it, but which is nonetheless present, and known to it. And ultimately it is this knowledge that matters, for it contains both the legitimation and, even more, the demand, that we never give up our inquiry into the spirit.

Joyce and the Present Age *(1936)* [1]

translated by Maria Jolas

FOR every creative man approaching his fiftieth year, there arises the question of his relation to the epoch in which he lives. From then on he is gradually eliminated from his own epoch, and with the appearance on the scene of young men of twenty-five, he has already begun to wonder whether he will or will not understand their generation. As the epoch which is still, but not for long, his own gradually becomes impregnated with a new kind of being and new problems, and he is faced with the ineluctability of growing old, it is at this point that he seeks proof as to whether his own work, which has developed within a given time and stems, at least as regards its basic elements, from his own youth, has assumed the status of reality, if considered apart from the magnificent, intoxicating play which accompanies each new swell of the wave of time as it casts up to the surface new colors, new forms: he seeks proof that it

[1] Maria Jolas, ed., *A James Joyce Yearbook* (Paris: Transition Press, 1949), pp. 68–108.

was not an evanescent play, but a reality that is firm and consistent as are all realities which have been produced by an epoch and have appeared at an appointed time, in which they are rooted; a reality that is sunk and is still sinking from its own weight into the waters of time, which cannot, however, wash it away, and in whose depths it lies gleaming, immortal, like the spirit of any given period, sometimes of a mere generation, making its influence vividly felt into the far distant future. Here then is the question, the knowledge, the hope, the anguish of the man of fifty, before which his personal problem of growing old becomes inexistent: if his work has really absorbed the spirit of the time, that is, to a degree which so far surpasses all the a priori, established "coloration" of the era that exists for every man and for all human activity, in short, so far surpasses the generally accepted "style of the time" that it represents an "expression" of the epoch (*nota bene:* an expression of it, not a photograph, as is given by the newspapers) — then this work belongs to the reality of the epoch, and fulfills with it that "historic reality" which is itself a guarantee of enduring beyond time.

Yet what does this historic reality consist of? What goes to make up a total reality of this kind, which guarantees to such a product of the imagination as the work of the poet, to such a mystic concept as that of the *Zeitgeist,* a historic dignity and an existence before which the so-called concrete vanishes into almost schematic unreality and impermanence? There is no need, in order to elucidate this point, to descend into the mystic; the mystic is never anything but man's urge to constitute a body of evidence, and man's faculty to attain to his great spiritual achievements is also mystic. For when all is said, the existence of the *Zeitgeist* is rooted in the concrete; it is built on the countless millions of anonymous yet concrete individual existences which people the epochs; it consists of the countless myriads of anonymous yet concrete individual force-units which give continuous impetus to the totality of events; and in the concrete wholeness of this inconceivably infinite, infinitely faceted "universal quotidian of the epoch" is to be found the *Zeitgeist,* is reflected its already nearly incomprehensible countenance. And the same concrete (or if preferred, even "naturalistic") totality appears in every great achievement of the intellect, but especially in every artistic achievement: having been either elected or prescribed in this respect by a special constellation of fate, its mission is to constitute the focal point of the anonymous powers of the epoch, to gather them in as though they were the *Zeitgeist* itself, to bring order into their chaos and thus to make them serve its own creation. This is a mythical task: mythical in the mystery of its accomplishment, mythical in its materialization, mythical in its symbolization of the mysterious forces at work in chaos, mythical in achievement and mythical in effect. Differing in just this respect from the anonymous, individual facets of the "universal quotidian of the epoch," which remain isolated and are affected only by this or that single force, which they also represent, great intellectual and artistic creation becomes therefore the immediate, concrete carrier of all the forces that influence the epoch — to be sure, with the concrete immediacy that is peculiar to genius and one of its principal criteria; it becomes the veritable re-creation of the epoch, which has potentially entered into it as well as into its elaboration; and in such intense, immediate harmony with the time, the work of art, the "universal work of art" becomes the mirror of the *Zeitgeist*.

Epochs that possess a strong inner nexus of values, particularly religious epochs, find their counterpart and that of their *Zeitgeist* in their institutions. They likewise absorb without friction, so to speak, the great intellectual and artistic achievements which, as their image and mirror of their mirror, originate in and stem from them. On the other hand, epochs in which there is decay of values lose this "inner" view of the presentation of self, they become "naturalistic"; but man can never grasp through "natural" means the totality in the innermost part of which he lives (supposing, of course, that such a thing as totality still exists); looked at from "within," to a certain extent the epoch assumes for him the appearance of being "organically unknowable"; and should he wish to comprehend it he must wait until he can survey it "from the outside"— that is, until it has become "historical," and having awakened to full historical reality and "efficacy," has revealed to him, along with its now visible totality, its *Zeitgeist* as well. (All epochs in which values are decayed are historically oriented.) Nowhere is this so manifest as in the great work of art which, being the mirror of the *Zeitgeist,* shares its destiny: the work of art shares, too, this state of being "organically unknowable" to its contemporaries — both *Faust* and the later works of Beethoven were received with incomprehension — and this incomprehensibility may in no way be attributed to the "novelty" of the work (the fashionably "new" is eagerly welcomed) nor to uneasiness in the face of "magnitude" (the great, universal works of the past are received with enthusiasm); it is due simply and solely to the sort of "anticipatory reality" which strikes contemporaries with "organic blindness," and only restores their vision — this usually occurs simultaneously with the arrival of a new generation, which also explains the significance of the fiftieth birthday for the artist — when the exterior aspect of the epoch has made its appearance and the epoch, the *Zeitgeist* and the work of art all become visible in their entirety. It is therefore not at all a question of the eye and ear "becoming accustomed" to the "abstruseness" of the work, as the current explanation of this "growth into time" would have it: around 1875, Wagner was a misesteemed wonder for the musical-minded; around 1900, however, for the unmusical-minded, who did not need to accustom themselves to anything, listening to him presented no problem; but we must not overlook the fact that this abstruseness is also rooted in the structural composition of the epoch itself, thus possessing, as does everything structural, an objective, even a very far-reaching significance. For, from this point on, the problem is simply one of "imitability": in epochs whose values are religiously centered, the "universal level" and with it, the quality level of art shows striking uniformity; a single "grand style" becomes evident which makes itself felt even in minor manifestations, and it is in this uniformity that all the forces of the epoch are oriented toward the collective order which they serve; however, the moment decay of these values sets in, this very uniformity is destroyed, and the further the fission of values progresses, and the more chaotic the distribution of world forces becomes in consequence, the greater, proportionately, will be the artistic expenditure necessary to the organizing and assembling of these various forces. Indeed, this expenditure becomes so great and so complicated that — in manifest opposition to epochs of genuine values — works of real magnitude within the general artistic production become not only more and more rare, but also more complex and inaccessible, before which fact the problem arises as to whether a world subject to the steadily increasing fission of values will not, in the end, be forced to forgo its total compre-hension through the work of art and thus become "unimitable." This question, which is extremely urgent for the artistic creation of the pres-ent time, can, however, only be answered through the work of art itself, provided that the latter — for this question too must be asked — prove to be a work of art that participates in totality and is truly attuned to the time.

IF WE apply this double standard — *sub speciae aeternitatis* and *sub spe-ciae mortis* — to the work of the fifty-year-old writer James Joyce, we find once more an entire series of the above-mentioned criteria, not the least of which is that of effectiveness on the fringe of the epoch. *Ulysses* became famous around 1930, with the appearance of a new generation; only this new generation succeeded in breaking through the state of being "organically unknowable" which had characterized the work until then, and the commonplace quotidian of Mr. Bloom, the hero of *Ulysses,* became the "universal quotidian" of the epoch of 1905; it was given to this new generation to sense all the anonymous forces of the epoch, the totality of which, having been caught up in the mirrors and counter-mirrors of Joyce's work, radiate from it as one, united and trans-formed to shed such powerful light that, in its rays, not only the figure of the hero but also the entire epoch and, consequently, the totality of being and man-being, are lighted up "from within"; meanwhile *Ulysses* strides mythically through the darkness of time and of the times. Both its inner and outer efficacy being attuned to the time, the *Ulysses* epic burst upon the evolution of the new literature with an "anticipatory reality" of real violence, and thus, despite its hermiticism, has already proven, at least from the standpoint of literary history (from this standpoint, the comparison between Joyce and Klopstock is justifiable), its capacity for outlasting time. But this contemporaneity is also expressed in another way; for the rationalism of the time, as exemplified by the intense urge toward self-awareness, is so significantly and emphatically manifested with Joyce, as is everything with this strangely gifted genius, that one might almost think the very symptoms of contemporaneity had been consciously generated: not only because a single concrete quotidian is chosen to represent the universal quotidian; not only because by setting the stage back to the year 1905, the generation is spanned exactly to the day; not only because the mythical mission of the work of art is demonstrated through a poetically prefigured homely event that is also emphasized by deliberate reference to history and allegory; not only all this, and much more. But it is also as though Joyce — and how could this be otherwise conceivable, in the case of so keen a mind as his! — had intended to adopt a definite position with regard to the possibility of imitating the world and to poetic creation in general. Through the complexity of his representational apparatus, through the almost rationally esoteric nature of his conceptual and linguistic processes (his word- and sentence-polyphony is rooted in some ten languages and constitutes, despite its astonishing flexibility, polish, precision and beauty, an almost aggressive dissolution of language), through the gigantic superstructure he has erected over the poetic immediacy that lies hidden beneath it, it is as though Joyce wanted to furnish proof (at the same time that he pursues the witty marginal aim of supporting the "organically unknowable") that it is precisely the success of this sort of enormous undertaking, precisely this kind of felicitous imitation of a world whose defiance of imitation may be imitated, precisely the hypertrophic power of expression to which the writer is driven, which makes it possible to express the inarticulateness of a world condemned to remain mute. It is as though, being himself profoundly shaken by this state of affairs, he wanted to strike up a superdimensional swan-song, and thus, to the accompaniment of one last, imposing poetic creation, reduce poetry itself *ad absurdum* and bury it once and for all. Was this his intention? The strong emotion emanating from this work leaves all that is rational and conscious well behind it — were this not the case the work would never have come into being — but this emotion is also colored by profound pessimism and aversion to all inherited and therefore already obsolete modes of being. It is colored with deep aversion to rational thinking which, though penetrating, has nothing left to say; to language, which, though beautiful, has lost its power of expression. In short, it is an emotion that springs from a loathing for culture — here too it is in tune with the time, for it is the loathing for rationality with which an overrationalized age plunges into the irrational — it is an emotion marked by the tragic cynicism with which modern man, desiring culture, nevertheless destroys it; it is an emotion in which Joyce negates not only his own artistic action, but art itself (which he constantly represents as an operatic buffoon); an emotion for which he feels he can find no outlet, no solution or release other than the purely animal, to be found in the gentle sleep of the body; an emotion which nevertheless has forced him to conceive things from a universal standpoint. Certainly no present-day artist can avoid this dilemma, none can escape pessimism with regard to his own activity. No one, however, has presented this conflict between the urge to create and the urge to destroy in so exemplarily significant and at the same time aggressive a manner as Joyce. And yet! However loudly he may proclaim that his poetically apprehended world is no longer apprehendable poetically, and that all former values must henceforth be dissolved in the muteness of the merely animal;

though he bring into play his entire artistic power with all its esotericism, complexity and richness, in defense of this opinion, though he sneer wryly at himself and his followers, and decree a break with art — this remains none the less his personal opinion, which must withdraw in favor of the work (strangely enough, this probably corresponds to Joyce's own wish). The work itself must speak, as must also its contemporaneity and universality; and thus the only thing possible is to examine and question the currents themselves that flow through the Joycean world-quotidian of the epoch: to what extent have they shaped and are they shaping the epoch, to what extent do they give it form and expression, to what extent may they themselves be identified with the spirit of the age and hence with the age itself?

The universal quotidian of the epoch that forms the content of Joyce's *Ulysses* epos is a quotidian taken from the life of Mr. Leopold Bloom, a quotidian from an average prewar life, whose connection with world-history is limited to the reading of newspapers. Mr. Bloom is a commonplace, somewhat comical gentleman of Jewish descent and Christian faith, who follows the more or less uncertain calling of advertising solicitor in the very provincial city of Dublin; and June 16th, 1905, the day on which we accompany him from nine o'clock in the morning until three o'clock the next morning, is a commonplace day in a commonplace life of this kind. Bloom's thoughts are commonplace, as are his relations with his fellow-men and with his competitors, who are also commonplace. Then there's his wife Molly, who deceives the worthy Bloom with very commonplace scruples, and has to deceive him because she's like that; commonplace, too, the citizens of the town, though there be a few odd fish among them; and commonplace even Bloom's counterpart, the idling, heedless, intellectual student, Stephen Dedalus. And nothing happens except that the man Bloom gets up in the morning, prepares breakfast for his wife Molly, starts off to work, attends a funeral, visits the public baths, takes his lunch, goes back to his business again, dines in a restaurant that evening, meets Stephen Dedalus, drags around alone on the beach, fastens his erotic desires on some girl or other, meets Dedalus again late that night, looks in on a bordel, and finally, with Dedalus, after they have drunk bad coffee in a cheap pub, ends up in his own house where they philosophize awhile before Dedalus leaves him and he himself lands in the marital bed. Sixteen hours of life in 1200 pages, sixteen hours of life during which, because nature has ordered it that way, the principal characters occasionally go to the toilet.

If it takes 1200 pages to describe sixteen hours of life, this makes 75 pages per hour, or more than a page for each minute, almost a line for each second; and as, in addition to this, the natural needs of men are accurately chronicled, one might suppose the essence of this book to be grandiloquent naturalistic recording. This naturalism undoubtedly exists, it exists very intensely even, and is in no way limited, as many seem to think, to psychological factors, or to the interior monologue, peculiar to Joyce; it comprises, in fact, every naturalistic method, from Zola to Dostoievsky, and even beyond. But this realistic, often sharply caricatural satiric portrait of Bloom, his antagonists and the city of Dublin in 1905, only forms the lower stratum of a much more fantastic picture; in fact, it is not even the lower but rather a sort of middle stratum, through which gleam the fantastic and the fabulous. A still-life by Snyder is merely naturalistic, whereas Rembrandt's slaughtered ox is more than naturalistic.

This denaturalization of naturalism might be regarded as primarily a problem of style; for it is always easier to grasp that which is formal, and with Rembrandt, too, one thinks first of problems of light and shade. It is indeed true that parallel with the continuous naturalism of *Ulysses,* as well as underneath and above it, there emerges every possible kind of style. It is not only that traditional forms of representation, that is, the epic, lyric and dramatic forms, are merged into one; not only that these are all diversely variegated through transformations which pass from scientific to Homeric expression, and that each of the twelve chapters of *Ulysses* is written in a different style; in fact, there are also passages in this book which might well be described as Expressionistic, passages in which the subject presented seems to be so broken up that it is easy to understand those critics who have mentioned Dadaistic influence. Of course one might deduce from the emergence of all these currents that distinguish and determine modern literature that Joyce is especially attuned to the time; but apart from the fact that this furnishes much too narrow a basis of evidence for so far-reaching a deduction, it might be argued that such an agglomeration of styles is merely the result of eclecticism. However, the extraordinary concentration with which all these instruments of style and forms of expression are gathered together into artistic unity; the truly symphonic mastery, ironic to a degree, with which they are utilized for the architectonic acceleration and slowing-up of events, weakens the charge of eclecticism or, more accurately, lifts it onto a plane of "creative" eclecticism. For it is only in a new form such as this that contemporaneity is demonstrated, only in new unity and togetherness, such as are to be found here, that the alloyed styles prove their vigor and justify their existence. To quote an example: Dadaism, or Futurism, undoubtedly had real significance in their time, but there is little point in discussing the content of their ideas or their eternal value. It will be quite a different thing, however, when Futuristic or Dadaistic elements come to be used as the basis of a man's complete works:[2] only then will they evidence their potentiality to become facets of the universe, which remains completely invisible so long as these researches are considered merely as isolated manifestations or make a claim to universality.

Viewed technically, Joyce's stylistic agglomeration is an experiment whereby the subject is lighted up first by one and then by another style, in order to exhaust its possibilities completely and to obtain from it the highest measure of reality, or rather, of super-naturalistic reality. Of course this cannot be compared with the musical *scherzo* which develops a theme in diverse stylistic manners, for here — and the concept of style generally assumes its proper significance only in such surround-

[2.] Broch's phrase, "Bausteine in einem Gesamt-kunstwerk," has been here infelicitously rendered. Broch speaks of building blocks in a total work of art, a synthesis of the arts, à la Wagner. —Ed.

ings — the subject has grown out of the style, and only through effect and counter-effect of this kind is a reality created which is the inner reality of the world. For everything significant comes into being as a result of reflection and symbols, and the original, genuine things are to be found quite as frequently at the end as at the beginning of the row of mirrors. Through recognition of this point — in this connection the recognition is a technical one — may be explained the fact that, in the case of Joyce, all problems of style are eventually brought under the domination of language. For his work presents a prevalence of the purely sonorous that is full of mystic significance, and to attribute this phenomenon to Joyce's musicality alone is as great a mistake as to speak of Dadaistic veneer, or to see no precedent other than the linguistic cult of George and his school. Nor is it a question of musical ornamentation, but rather of a certain fundamental quality in which the ultimate symbol of expression becomes language per se, the magic quality of sound that is the culmination of every chain of similes and has grown mystically from remote origins, to which it returns — the beginning and end of each chain of symbols, yet visible in each connecting link, for the reason that there is nothing in the most varied chains of symbols that is not at the same time a connecting link. It is surely permissible to regard this exceedingly complicated and subtle technique — this fluctuating experience of a fluctuating reality, this continuous intermarriage of the most diverse chains of symbols, this continuous smelting of these chains in the medium of language, which constitutes at the same time the most tangible result of the smelting — as the very core of Joyce's descriptive art. The technique of the *leitmotif,* for example, which Joyce employs with such manifold and infinite variation, should by no means be confused with that of Wagner, although as a musician, Joyce may have borne this in mind. It is rather what might be described as a natural consequence of the tangled chains of symbols which necessarily produce a criss-cross of recurrent motifs, thus demonstrating not only the dual and multiple unity of place and language-sense, but also the simultaneity of all these chains of symbols. In fact, there is constant concern with simultaneity, as well as with the parallelism of the infinite possibilities presented by the splitting up of everything that has symbolic content, and one feels throughout an effort to imprison and bind the infinitude of the incomprehensible that envelopes the world and constitutes its reality, with chains of symbols that so far as possible must be given simultaneous expression. And though this striving for simultaneity (which is also indicated by the compression of events into a single day) cannot avoid the necessity of expressing the contiguous and the interwoven by means of the successive, or the unique by means of repetition, the demand for simultaneity remains nevertheless the real objective of all that is epical, in fact of all that is poetic. This objective may be defined as follows: to unify a succession of impressions and experiences, to force the current back into the unity of the simultaneous, to relegate time-conditioned elements to the timelessness of the monad; in short, to establish the supratemporal nature of the work of art in the concept of indivisible homogeneity.

Joyce has met this challenge with all his thoroughness and unstinting pains, and it goes without saying that the means for attaining such a goal are not exhausted by the principle of change of style, nor by that of linguistic renewal, nor by the technique of chains and intermarriage of symbols. All we have said thus far on the subject constitutes merely a kind of longitudinal section through Joyce's method of symbolic representation, whereas the cross-section reveals an entirely different and essentially more direct symbolic presentation of meaning: for there is hardly a situation in *Ulysses* which does not possess, alongside its naturalistic significance, numerous others as well. This is most readily characterized as esoteric-allegorical experiment. It is not for nothing that the work is called *Ulysses,* for Bloom's wanderings through the city of Dublin constitute an odyssey which repeats in a new disguise the journey of the noble sufferer Odysseus, with all its episodes. But this allegory would be a mere jest if it did not possess deeper spiritual significance, if it did not itself contain an allegory raised to the *n*th degree, if we did not find in it once more the essence of life and of all that is poetic, for which Homer stands. It is an allegorical structure and super-structure that pertains as well to the primitive functions of life as to ultimate philosophical-scholastic considerations; an allegorical cosmogony in which, moreover, Ireland and its history are raised to the position of a world allegory, a cosmogony possessing such wealth of strata and such complexity that it could only have been created by a poly-historical and theological mind such as that of Joyce, but which also needed for its understanding an extensive commentary such as that of Stuart Gilbert.

Is this another technical problem? Certainly not, although, from the author's viewpoint, each representational problem must be a technical one and the understanding of each new work is most easily arrived at by way of its technical genesis. In somewhat simplified outline it might be said that Joyce's method comprises in its longitudinal section a formal and functional symbolization; in its cross-section, however, the symbolization is one of content and statics. But such divisions, despite their simplification, are for the most part ill-defined, since content and form always converge. It is precisely this question of dual, threefold, manifold simultaneity, so evident in *Ulysses,* which shows how the bonds of form and pure technique are ultimately burst asunder. We are faced here with what may be described as an inner simultaneity. For the story of Bloom-Ulysses is not only progression in time, it is also action, perfectly definite action, which involves Bloom and a number of other characters. The story of Dedalus, the second protagonist, often runs on quite independently of Bloom, and Bloom's inner monologue is frequently relieved by that of the persons who play opposite him; the entire last chapter consists of the inner monologue of his wife, Molly. Soon, however, we become aware that all these persons are caught up in a single current, and that although, to be sure, each has his own life, they nevertheless belong together in a closely-knit whole. And this whole is represented by Bloom, it is Bloom, and beyond Bloom it is mankind in general. It would be permissible to speak of Bloom's different selves, of selves which reflect each other reciprocally as in a dream, and if we were to attempt to explain this naturalistically, it might be said that intimate relations are only established between persons who partake each of the other's self. Thus Bloom's wife, Molly, whose life is one of bald instinct, embodies his most obscure, most brutish humanity, while his reason is manifested in Dedalus, who incarnates his spiritual son. This becomes absolutely clear in the brothel scenes, in which Bloom's soul sheds all its inhibitions and his unshackled phantasy attains concrete identity with all his imagined selves. This is the dramatic climax of the work — it is significant that the very form should narrow down to that of the drama — all the chains of symbols converge, the leitmotifs knot into a compact mass, and the different strata of allegorical representation pile up on top of each other. It is the climax of a technique of simultaneity which is more than a technique, and which runs through the entire work, giving constant proof that it is the universality of life and of mankind that is in question, a universality whose expression extends from the deepest irrational stratum up to the most rational thinking processes of the work. This is obtained not only by overlaying the different styles (Molly's monologue is nothing but the unpunctuated stringing together of instinctive molluscous associations; the conversations of Dedalus assume the stiffened form of a rigid catechism, the ultimate ossification of theology), but also through the action itself, in the domain of which — that of human relations — the problem of artistic unity and simultaneity is once more projected. But in this case it has almost ceased to be a problem, and neither naturalistic interpretation of the course of the event, nor considerations on the subject of artistic technique, succeed in reaching into that deepest zone in which perfection and the genuinely epistemological significance of art are inherent; this is a question of the Platonic ideality of events whose simultaneity is determined solely through the "I," through an "I" which in this special case to be sure is named Bloom, but which ultimately is the general "I," or simply the human.

This is certainly of great importance. Meanwhile, we have under-taken to discuss Joyce's contemporaneity and to explain it through the abstruseness and isolation of his work. Its difficulties are probably by now quite evident, although little has been done other than to point out the resemblance of certain stylistic peculiarities to those that exist in numerous literary currents of recent years. Can it be that this contem-poraneity must be looked for in the Platonism of *Ulysses?* One would be more inclined to believe that in this instance we are faced with a highly personal atavism, a left-over from Joyce's Catholic-theological school-ing, a theism from which God has been banished; banishment of God, however, being its only modern aspect, since it is rooted in a purely medieval pattern and technique of thinking.

However, one could just as well assert the contrary. For if such a thing as contemporaneity exists at all, it cannot be dependent on choice of theme, that is to say the Platonic or non-Platonic theme. It must derive from a certain state of consciousness, from a certain state of logic, in short from a certain technique of thought; from a form of logic which is binding for the period concerned, and which therefore leads automati-cally to its themes and to their peculiar content. But the question is far from being one of content. When Gide, for example, uses the novel as the narrative framework for psychoanalytical or other scientific digres-sion, it does not mean that modernity has been attained; this would only be the case if the spirit of scientific thinking—under its specifically rational form of causative agent—were to penetrate all the remaining purely poetic portrayal. For then it is a matter of indifference whether scientific themes are treated at all, the theme simply becomes the func-tion of the poetic; and if this were not true the scene of the modern novel would have to be laid exclusively among scholars, or else against the background of cultural disorder which, as a matter of fact, characterizes many of the more recent social novels. *Ulysses* certainly does not lack scholarliness, and many will even find it overburdened in this respect: we might mention in passing, however, that it can also be considered as a psychoanalytical novel, not only because of the prevailing father-son problem (Bloom between the father Virag and the son Dedalus), but also because of the profound correspondence between the form of the inner monologue and the free-association method used in psychoanalytical therapy. However, scholarship never becomes an aim in itself, but continues to be merely a method of representation that has nothing at all to do with so-called scientific content. And that Joyce should reject psychoanalysis — which is evidenced by a number of his utterances — only confirms the above statement, only proves that the relation between his thinking and that of psychoanalysis is merely one of method, function of a super-individual, methodical logicity, to which both the novel and psychology are objective, which is the *Zeitgeist* and which forces man to descend into the meta-logical regions of the unconscious and the irrational, to track down the primal moving elements of being, in order that against such a background sphere of experience and reality he may reveal and recognize himself in the fearful but magnificent nexus between animal and god which he prefers not to see but which he constitutes, none the less. One might almost say that an unbroken line leads in geometrical simultaneity from the depths of Molly's associations to the theological dialectics of Dedalus; and in between, belonging to both of them, he himself both, is Bloom.

Examples such as these exist in great number. Just to mention one more, *Ulysses* certainly has nothing to do with the theory of relativity, nor is there a single mention of it in the book. Yet we might prove with reason that the epistemological substance of the theory of relativity is given in the discovery of the logical medium within the physical sphere of observation. This can be explained in the following manner: classical physics was content to observe and measure the phenomena to be explored, and it paid attention to the observational medium, to the act of seeing, only in so far as the latter developed sources of error — either through insufficiency of the human sense organs, or through that of our measuring instruments. But the theory of relativity has revealed that in addition to this, there exists a basic source of error, namely, the act of seeing in itself, the act of observing per se, so that, consequently, in order to avoid this source of error, both the observer and his act of seeing — an ideal observer and an ideal act of seeing — must be drawn into the field of observation; in short, that for this, theoretical unity of the physical object and the physical act of seeing must be established. It can give no offense to the theory of relativity if we draw a parallel with literature; the classical novel was satisfied with the observation of the real and the psychic circumstances of life, and it was satisfied to describe these by means of language. The only challenge to be met was that of seeing a portion of nature through a temperament. These writers described something and for this they used language as an immutable instrument handed down to them as such. What Joyce does, however, is essentially more complicated. With him there is concurrent recognition that it is not permissible simply to place the object under observation and do nothing other than describe it; but that representation of the subject, in other words "the narrator as idea," and not the least the language with which he describes the representational object, belong to it in the role of representational media. What he seeks to create is a unity of representational object and representational means, in the most far-reaching sense of the word, a unity which sometimes gives the impression that the object has been overpowered by language, and language by the object, to the point of utter exhaustion, but which nevertheless remains a unity, avoiding all superfluous padding as well as all superfluous epithets; a unity in which one thing grows naturally out of another, for the reason that in its wholeness it is subject to the systemization of knowledge. The title of his new work, "Work in Progress," work that is advancing, work that is in process of becoming, work that is developing, divulges this purpose. The work must develop of itself out of observation, and the observer is always right in the midst of it, he is presenting something and, at the same time, representing himself and his labor. The following may be taken as a relatively simple example of the contents of the chapter, *Anna Livia Plurabelle:* as always with Joyce, this name has numerous other meanings and the heroine, Anna Livia, has a mysterious and yet very rational connection with the river Liffey, that flows through the city of Dublin. Two washerwomen are kneeling on the bank of the river, washing dirty clothes. Across the water they are exchanging bits of gossip about the town and about the heroine, Anna Livia Plurabelle. Their conversation continues to the rhythm of their washing, with its rubbing and beating. In fact, their conversation is itself washing, for the reason that they are washing the dirty linen of the whole town. But as darkness falls and the mist lowers, the conversation lags and the movements of the washerwomen slacken; the river grows wider and wider in the deepening mist, its murmur becomes more and more audible. The murmur of the river intrudes upon the conversation, for nothing is described, everything originates in and out of the talk of the washerwomen who have now ceased to be washerwomen, but have become fabulous beings, one the stem of a shrub on the bank, the other a piece of stone, both lapped by the swelling waves, and their talk finally nothing but the dying murmur of the river, incomprehensible to the listener, incomprehensible to themselves, music of the water, embodied in human sound, which is scarcely speech any longer. And if I may make a personal confession, I find it indescribably beautiful.

Perhaps this will suffice to show the relationship of Joyce's method with the position of science and with the peculiar logicity which has led to this position. It may also have become clear, from the example of *Anna Livia Plurabelle,* how, starting in this case from the problem of medium, there follows the extremely curious dissolution of the object which, at the same time, is a precise outline of it and finds its analogy only in the dissolution of physical matter through mathematical functions, as demonstrated in the case of modern physics. But for those who are not yet convinced of the circumstantial proof of Joyce's contemporaneity, a further parallel phenomenon, and not the least, might be cited; namely, that of the plastic arts. For the fact that they may be looked at has always resulted in a sort of style essence that situates the cultural epoch intellectually.

Certain it is that events, past or present, in the world of painting constitute only a small and at the same time increasingly gross part of what happens in the domain of the intellect. But it is precisely the increasing evidence of this grossening into visibility that explains why visitors to the Paris salon of 1863 went into a rage before the paintings of Manet. This was a perfectly legitimate defensive reaction. For what was evident there — and people began to feel it at the time — was the revolutionary sign of a definitive change of the *Zeitgeist* and, as many were inclined to prophesy, the end of art. Under the pretext of being obliged to introduce physical-optical knowledge into the technique of painting, a development was inaugurated which alienated painting from its original aim of representing the object, in order to seek a junction with the *Zeitgeist* and its presumed scientific proclivities in the name and with the help of technical painting problems. What emerged here was faith in science and in scientific progress in general, the specific faith of the 19th century; and the fact that art turned to symbolization of the new faith was a belated, unconscious imitation of the medieval artist who worked exclusively in the service of his faith. However far from exact such comparisons may be, if we consider the dissolution of the object which has taken place in the domain of modern physics, it may nevertheless be noted that further evolution of modern art led to complete absence of the object in *Suprematism,* as well as to a purely ornamental art, and that what happened subsequently presented similar aspects: now whether *Expressionism* was searching for purely emotional motives, that is, objectless emotions in the subject, in order to raise them to the position of what was in fact the original object of painting; whether *Futurism* strove to seize the object cinematographically in purely functional movement as representing dissolution of the spatial world; or whether *Cubism* — it was almost a return to the past — simply initiated the search for the abstract object which it hoped to discover in a fixed set of laws governing the painter's craft and the formation of space — it was in each case a matter of replacing the accidental, empirical object by one whose deepest roots would reach into the logical as well as into the Platonic idea, all of which was a consequence of the action of the *Zeitgeist,* since we may assume with certainty that the painter was unaware of these concepts. We have already indicated the parallel, albeit less accentuated stylistic tendencies of the simultaneous literary currents and their re-emergence in Joyce's work; thus we need not return to them. We shall merely point out that in painting, *Expressionism,* with its cult of the "I," had necessarily to be followed by an irruption of the irrational and its accompanying irrational symbolic forms, and that because the scale of possibilities of human expression is limited, there occurred a reversion to the abstract symbolic art of the primitive, toward which all ornamentalism tends, in any case. This might be called a reintroduction of the object into the work of art, only with a different signature, the naturalistic having been subjected to a change of key when the reality of the object became merely the representative of the abstract, destined to carry out its demands. It is for this reason too that the object may be violated and distorted, and although this distortion is often at the service of a superior architectonics, and makes it possible to avoid padding, at the same time it legitimizes a satirical tendency which, although it stems from other sources, undoubtedly exists in modern art and mocks to the point of caricature the former notion of the object in repose. The way has been cleared for all kinds of eclectic research — here we may also speak of a productive eclecticism — and this research is by no means limited to primitive and exotic art, but derives the matter of its expression from all epochs of style, especially the classical, thus making it possible to produce through infinite crossings and smeltings with expressionistic and constructivistic principles, the network of successive symbols which, together, are presented by the complicated figure we know as "modern painting." On the other hand, if we examine the meager optical theory on which early impressionism was based, we see clearly the sum of theoretical and practical technical knowledge which the modern painter requires in order to dominate all the problems of his art; a knowledge that constitutes, in fact, a universality to which only one man — Picasso — has attained. For we should have to go well back into the history of painting, as far back perhaps as the great masters of the Renaissance, in order to duplicate — on another level, of course — the multiple means of expression, the mastery of existing techniques, the application of theory and science to the painter's art, that are to be found in the work of Picasso; and should we seek to attach a name in modern literature to a similar example of wealth, a similar abundance of metamorphous disso-lution and synthesis of the object, there exists really but one name, that of James Joyce.

We might also point to modern music which — being in a like situa-tion — has on the one hand acquired, through atonality, quite new so-called scientific bases and, on the other, reaches back toward pseudo-ancient and other historical styles, as well as to primitive and exotic forms. However, further discussion would appear unnecessary, all the more so since, in each case, there is the following most important, increasingly urgent question to be answered; can such art as this, which is entirely devoted and subject to its own technical problems; can such production, which is simply and solely a matter of art for art's sake; can such estheticism, whether of language or color, in other words, and to be brutally frank, can ornamentalism of this kind justify its claim to exis-tence? And is it not true that the introduction of scientific research into art has resulted in a merely apparent timeliness, one which in reality has to do with science, and science alone? For symbolization of the divine in medieval painting is certainly quite different from artistic representation of the scientific spirit, which, by its very nature, is an end in itself and needs no artistic representation. But even if we assume the existence of timeliness in art, this can be at most only a precondition, and guarantees neither its right to existence nor its survival. A conclusion may also be timely, in fact it must be so in order for it to be a genuine conclusion, and it is precisely the state of modern painting, despite Picasso, that confirms this point. For painting has become a completely esoteric, speculative affair, itself and its problems without interest for the majority of persons. In fact it is little more than the left-over of a past epoch, and though to be addicted to it is something of a personal misfortune, it is hardly any longer the tragedy of the artist who is unable to do otherwise. But isn't it also evident that in an epoch dominated by the dissolution of values each of the arts loses the justification of its existence? Isn't what has happened to the plastic arts the fate of writing as well? For not only has art in general been banished into its world of art for art's sake; not only has it been widely eliminated from the bourgeois system for countless reasons, the most important of which are economic, but this system itself is apparently either on the verge of dissolution, or in process of such profound transformation, as a result of capitalistic methods, that it has lost all resemblance to the formerly nutritive soil from which art has drawn its greatest vitality since the time of the schism of values that took place during the Renaissance. As a result, the bourgeoisie, which was once the social habitat of art, is this no longer, and art today is a social outcast. Why should literature, then, which is more deeply rooted in the social system from which it stems, more closely related to it — the great social novels of the nineteenth century are proof of this — be endowed with greater capacity for survival than any of the other arts? A world in which art is given social classification offers — precisely in the manner of its organization — not only certain guarantees for the artistic possibilities of its representation, but also confers a (social) representational obligation on the artist; and inversely, it might be said that when this representational obligation no longer exists, the power to represent and indeed, in the final analysis, representability itself, cease to exist. To be sure, it might also be asserted that social conditions constitute only a minor factor in the great problem of representability and that, for the artist, there exists a supra-social representational obligation which continues to exert an influence — universal works such as those of Picasso or

Joyce give evidence of this — even in the social, economic and linguistic isolation of art for art's sake. Yet even if this assertion were true, the supra-social representational obligation would lead, at best, to purely personal creation on the part of the artist, which commits him to nothing so long as it does not also involve a supra-social commitment that has general implications; so long, in other words, as there does not exist for art a supra-social functional importance. In the case of the plastic arts, this functional importance would now appear to have become hardly provable; but is the claim of literature any more valid? Can *Ulysses* (which contains a more somber picture of the relation of the bourgeoisie to art) make such a claim? Is literature obliged to represent something in which there also emerges the representability of the object? Does literature fulfill a function which leads beyond the frontiers of the ominous art for art's sake into the domain of the supra-social general commitment?

Here it is a question of the function of cognition, which is essentially free, from the social point of view. In fact, all truly artistic activity is drenched in cognition and all genuine artistic apperception of universality undoubtedly denotes an act of eminent intellectual cognition — if this assumption of infinity were not behind all art, there would be no art. But in addition, in the case of literature, this cognitional task is transposed into yet another sphere (the Dedalus sphere in *Ulysses!*) according to material and means, and this second, rational sphere (which is socially uncommitted, like the student Dedalus) is related to the sphere of philosophical cognition in such a way — and in a manner approaching identity (as with Plato, who is really Bloom's ideal) — that it is obliged to take over from philosophy all those attributes which although properly philosophical, can no longer be elaborated upon by philosophy, for the reason that the latter, since its separation from theological circles, is deprived of its real argumentation and thus forced to withdraw to themes that are increasingly "scientific" and "exact." And it is just this (here too, beside the data of science itself, one might quote

Dedalus again) which is now increasingly the case. Apart from the fact that empirical natural science has been obliged to abandon its belief in the omnipotence of the causal principle, and that even the bases of mathematics have become unstable; quite apart from the fact, too, that positivism, in the naïve, original form in which it still believed it possible to attain a sort of religious, theological demonstration that would completely summarize scientific findings, has long since recognized failure and changed its position, it so happens that German idealism, which might be called the last late-blooming of the dialectical-theological spirit, the ultimate phase of pure philosophy for the sake of philosophizing, has taken cognizance of the frontier-limits of its own scholarliness: with all its faith in the primacy of the logos, philosophy knows that logic cannot so easily embrace universality, it knows that even the scant "condition of possible experience," to which Kant limited the task of the theory of knowledge, is dependent on the scientifically comprehensible as such; it knows that logical verification can advance only by degrees, for the reason that only that which can be mathematically formulated may be called scientific and demonstrable. Thus philosophy has frequently returned to pure logic, but although it clings now as before to its basic philosophical standpoint, it has nevertheless felt constrained to eliminate certain attributes — particularly the ethical and the metaphysical — from its domain. The age of philosophical universality, which was also the age of the great compendiums, was brought to an end by philosophy itself, which became obliged to withdraw its most burning questions from the realm of logical discussion or else, as Wittgenstein has put it, refer them back to the mystical.

It is at this point that the mission of literature begins; the mission of a cognition that remains above all empirical or social modes of being and to which it is a matter of indifference whether man lives in a feudal, bourgeois or proletarian age; literature's obligation to the absoluteness of cognition, in general.

It is quite possible, probable even, that Goethe had a premonition of this development. Otherwise, the fact that as the contemporary of Kant, Fichte and Schelling, as well as the friend of the Kantian Schiller, he did not establish relationship with Kant's philosophy, is inexplicable. Nor is it possible to explain otherwise that he, whose scientific interests may be rightly called universal, should have regarded the tendency to scientific specialization with near-hatred. These negations have been exploited often enough by the most diverse world-concepts, and numerous are the types of hazy thinking that have sought to erect their Goethe memorial in the shadow of the great man. He who rejected speculative theology became "the great pagan," as a poet he was branded the scorner of strict cognition, the curiously tempestuous "universal man," to whom the loose concept "life" was all that mattered; while his rejection of Kant's philosophy won him the title of the first positivist. And because he dubbed himself a dilettante, dilettantism everywhere chose him as its patron. What blasphemy! And it continues even today. Nobody has understood more clearly than Goethe to what extent poetic creation is rooted in the problem of cognition, no one ever made the choice in favor of literature with a greater sense of responsibility. His dilettantism was that of the man who finds satisfaction in no special science and who strives to attain to the totality of all knowledge. It was also the enormous, deeply serious responsibility of the scholar who, having broken through and exceeded the rational frontiers of cognition, starts out in search of something that can be furnished neither by the speculative theories of theology or philosophy, nor by the so-called real cognition of exact science. His was the knowledge and well-founded skepticism of the responsible man who anticipated what was to become fact a hundred years later: it was also knowledge of the real aims of his own will to cognition, directed toward the mystical residue to be found in all experience, toward the higher reality which overshadows all external-positivistic reality, as well as toward genuine metaphysical cognition, to exalt which was the true, the essential, the supra-bourgeois goal of Goethe's creative lyricism.

This will of the lyrical toward cognition, presented as function of the all-embracing effort toward cognition, might be called impatience for cognition, out-distancing rational cognition, which only advances step by step toward totality, without ever reaching it. But it is precisely this totality that is the mission of art and literature, their basic mission even, and the impatience for cognition that is expressed in lyricism is not only the justified impatience of earth-bound man, who sees death ahead of him, but genuine religious impatience as well. For that which is religious inevitably reaches out toward totality of cognition, is inevitably aware of the brevity of human existence and seeks to fill our brief existence with the totality of cognition.

At the side of the truly religious man, as also at that of the creator, there is always death, exhorting him to fill his life with ultimately attainable significance, in order that it may not have been lived in vain. If there exists a justification of literature, or a supra-temporality of artistic creation, it is to be found in a totality of cognition such as this. For the totality of world comprehension as striven for by the work of art, in Goethe's sense at least, concentrates all knowledge of humanity's endless evolution into one simultaneous act of cognition: eternity must be comprised in a single existence, in the totality of a single work of art, and the nearer the work of art comes to the frontiers of totality, the greater its possibility of survival. In this highest sense, the artist creates not only for the diversion and instruction of his public but purely and simply for the cultivation of his own existence. This is culture as Goethe understood it, in the form in which he opposed it to philosophy and the sciences; the hard, severe task of cognition which he never abandoned throughout his entire life, and which impelled him to voracious absorption of all the phenomena of life in order that, in the true sense of the word, he might transform them. It is this totality of existence which urged him on to absolutely new forms of expression, and in the *Wander Years,* laid the foundation stone of what was to be the new poetry and novel. But it is also adequate totality of form, that is, complete mastery of all esthetic forms of expression subjected to universality of content, as exemplified in *Faust,* which burst asunder all existing theatrical forms.

The responsibility which Goethe places on the shoulders of the writer is a gigantic one. It was to lie dormant for a hundred years, for the reason that the old values still held good and there was still hope that the burning questions concerning the soul might be satisfied from the perspective of theology and philosophy. Today this hope has faded. Philosophy and science have themselves become converted to a skepticism similar to that of Goethe, and they have abandoned all attempt to find answers to these burning questions. And yet the latter are quite as pertinent as they ever were. In Goethe's time the old values still obtained; and although he belonged to his time, his premonitions and knowledge were a century in advance. Those who came after him, born of their time and caught up as they were in their own epoch, even when they possessed the urge to universality of a Balzac or a Zola, or the will to form of a Flaubert, nevertheless still limited themselves, in fact they had to do so, to writing for the entertainment and instruction of their public. This is no longer possible today, since the spirit of the epoch has ceased to tolerate it. Today the writer is compelled to accept the challenge of Goethe and to assume the responsibility of the heritage handed down to him by humanity's striving for cognition. This heritage is the metaphysical, ethical problem, in other words it is the philosophical penetration of "existence" into the universality of world representation.

It would be absolutely false if we were to conclude from the foregoing that today's artistic production, even when it attains to its greatest stature, might be compared and measured with that of Goethe. Goethe was of his time, and today is today. And from a certain point of view it is perfectly comprehensible that to many readers the literature of the 19th century might possibly appear to more closely resemble that of Goethe than does *Ulysses;* or that the latter might be conceived of rather as being a bold attack on everything we are accustomed to associate with Goethe. But even if we make abstraction of all time-conditioning in the case of

Goethe, or shall we say, of everything that was bourgeois about him; even if we recognize in his striving for totality the only powerful challenge that points beyond the bourgeois epoch into all future time, this does not mean that today the only work of art that may be considered contemporary is one which completely meets this challenge. It is no more legitimate to take the demand for Faustian totality of form as the sole measuring-rod for present-day writing, than to insist that each new work be invested with Goethe's universality and resemble *Wilhelm Meister*. This would be a dreadful consistency. And although the nature of this age is one of radicalism, it is still only the exceptional writers of the age — and Joyce is one of them — who with this radicalism attain absolute breakthroughs. But regardless of the fact that modern literature can comply with Goethe's injunction only with the feeblest efforts at approximating it, still in one respect it must comply even in its most minor works, if it is to be worthy of the current age; and this one requirement has universal validity: namely, to raise literature to the plane of cognition; and, in the final analysis, this is an ethical task.

If we were to state that the age of the ethical work of art has dawned and that Goethe inaugurated it, this might sound like a slogan. And if all we meant were that the work of art must be taken out of the esthetic category and placed in that of the ethical, this too would mean very little: for it has always been the standpoint of the artist to create something good rather than something beautiful, and those who worked toward beauty alone, have always inevitably ended in kitsch. But it is in the nature of the bourgeois, or rather the philistine outlook, which is older than the bourgeois and will probably outlive it, to regard the work of art as a means of enjoyment, as a purely esthetic creation whose ultimate ideal derives from kitsch. This corruption of all that is artistic may also be symptomatic of the decay of culture, or possibly it is the return of ethical severity which is the sign of a new form of culture. It is a turning away from the pathos of the beautiful and turning toward the simple pathos of experience; from the pathos of tragedy to the suffering comedy of the human creature and cognition of his existence; from the pathos of the theatrical disguise to the higher reality which is rooted in man's inner being. The tragical hero has been relieved of the tragedy of earthbound creatures. And this ethical transformation may be sensed not only in a work of art of the stature of *Ulysses*, but in all artistic production. Now whether this ethical will tra-verse the artistic creation of our age to an ever-increasing degree in the form of satirical or comical diversion, and reaching even into music and the plastic arts, seek to re-establish contact with society; or whether the ethical deteriorates into political and other propagandistic art, that is, into mere moralizing, the work of art without an ethical aim is no longer valid; the writer is no longer permitted just to write, to be the poet and nothing else. And wherever and under whatever circumstances the work of art may be considered a genuine work of art, it bears within itself the principle of the formation of being, in its ultimate derivation it is still the expression of the will to cognition which is demanded by the spirit.

It is almost as though literature had been obliged to go through all the hells of art for art's sake before it could undertake the extraordinary task of bringing all esthetic elements under the dominion of the ethical; almost as though all the old value associations had really had to be experienced completely, in order that the comical—a component that was lacking in Goethe's totality—might develop out of the decay of the pathetic. For this new seriousness, this new metaphysics, the ethical work of art itself—all this new responsibility of the writer—had to be preceded by generalized dissolution, as well as by the most profound skepticism, which relates it back not only to Goethe, but to Kant. Joyce has taken all this enormous responsibility on his shoulders. To be sure, *Ulysses* is not a cultural novel in Goethe's sense, its only common feature being that it presumes the most extensive culture and the most fundamental universality on the part of the author. But since the ethical—

unless it remain bogged in dogmatic moralizing — must be rooted in a system that functions above it, and since the satirical and the comical, if they are to rise to a superior, effective sphere, must be rooted in totality of being; since, too, this totality can only be envisaged and determined from the perspective of the "I," or shall we say outright, from the perspective of transcendental consciousness — for these reasons the work of art, which has assumed full responsibility for the new task of cognition, must determine once and for all its logical place in this last sphere of the "I," that is, in the sphere of cosmic humor. This is the sphere of the Platonic and thus of the philosophic, in general. It is therefore absolutely necessary that the new philosophical cosmogony to which Joyce aspires with all the resources of his masterly style and architectonics, with absolute insight and all his irony, that this cosmogony, which is deployed behind *Ulysses,* should eventually result in a Platonic system, a cross-section of the world which, however, is nothing other than a cross-section of the "I," an "I" that is at once the *sum* and the *cogito,* at once the logos and life, reunited; a simultaneity in whose unity may be seen the glow of the religious per se.

We do not know whither Joyce's path will lead. The dangers of increasing aloofness are real and are to be found both in his pessimism and in the power of the artistic resources he has placed at the service of this pessimism. For the nearer he comes to the goal of a totality in which he does not believe, the narrower and more restricted becomes the net of symbols and associations in whose multiplicity all existence is to be imprisoned; and the more fundamentally the work of art undertakes the task of totality, without believing in it, the more threatening the peril of the infinite becomes; the infinite and death are children of one mother. And yet, although these dangers may also not be ignored as regards Joyce's future work; indeed, even though his pessimism should become still more justified with the further evolution of the world, and even though the scission of values should become increasingly great; even though the world quotidian should enter into a state of still greater confusion, and what is more, even though man should choose to turn completely away from cognition — this point has not yet been reached—cognition as such could not be impugned. For it is cognition which, again and again, at least potentially, injects into all destruction and decay of values, no matter how hopeless they may appear, the power to realize a transformation through new dispositions, the germ of a new religious organization of humanity. And since this is the case, literature may not relinquish its task of contemplating and symbolizing the forces of the age; an ethical task of cognition which becomes greater as man's longing to escape from imprisonment in the darkness of the annihilation of values increases. For at the end of the path may be seen the new mythos growing out of a world in formation. Whether or not this be realized, lyrical creation remains beyond both optimism and pessimism, its very existence even, is equivalent to optimism, and the fact that there exists a work of the artistic and ethical magnitude of *Ulysses* contributes to this optimism — even though it be in contradiction to the will of its author.

The Style of
the Mythical Age

(1947)[1]

SOMEWHERE in this book Rachel Bespaloff says: "It is impossible to speak of an Homeric world or a Tolstoyan world in the sense one can speak of a Dantesque world, a Balzacian or a Dostoievskian world. Tolstoy's universe, like Homer's, is what our own is from moment to moment. We do not step into it; we are there." This is a somewhat startling statement; and when we ask why it should be valid, one reason seems to us especially relevant: Homer is on the threshold where myth

---

[1.] This essay, written by Broch in English, was originally the introduction to Rachel Bespaloff's *On The Iliad,* translated from the French by Mary McCarthy (New York: Pantheon, 1948). An author and philosopher, Bespaloff emigrated to the United States in 1942 from Hyères, France, and taught French literature at Mount Holyoke College. She committed suicide in 1949. Broch's essay was edited by Jean Starr Untermeyer, who had translated *The Death of Virgil.* The favorable reception of the essay by the Bollingen Foundation led to Broch's writing the introduction to its Hofmannsthal edition, *Selected Prose* (New York: Pantheon, 1952), which eventually led to the book-length essay *Hugo von Hofmannsthal and His Time.* — Trans.

steps over into poetry, Tolstoy on that where poetry steps back into myth.

Coming from myth, returning to myth: the whole, or nearly the whole, history of European literature is strung between Homer and Tolstoy. But what a strange development of the human expression, since, apparently, it returns to its mythical source. Is this not like a late homecoming? And if it be such — does it not portend the dusk before the night? Is it not the curve that drops back into childhood?

Undoubtedly myth embraces qualities of both periods, that of childhood (so nearly identical with that of primitive man) and that of old age, the styles of both expressing the essential and nothing but the essential, the one before it has entered the realm of subjective problems, the other when it has left this realm behind.

The "style of old age" is not always a product of the years; it is a gift implanted along with his other gifts in the artist, ripening, it may be, with time, often blossoming before its season under the foreshadow of death, or unfolding of itself even before the approach of age or death: it is the reaching of a new level of expression, such as the old Titian's discovery of the all-penetrating light which dissolves the human flesh and the human soul to a higher unity; or such as the finding by Rembrandt and Goya, both at the height of their manhood, of the metaphysical surface which underlies the visible in man and thing, and which nevertheless can be painted; or such as the *Art of the Fugue* which Bach in his old age dictated without having a concrete instrument in mind, because what he had to express was either beneath or beyond the audible surface of music; or such as the last quartets of Beethoven, in which he — only then in his fifties but already near to death — found the way from earthly music to the music of the infinite; or such as Goethe's last writings, the final scenes of *Faust* for instance, where the language discloses its own mysteries and, therefore, those of all existence.

What is common to these various examples? All of them reveal a radical change in style, not merely a development in the original direction;

and this sharp stylistic break can be described as a kind of *abstractism* in which the expression relies less and less on the vocabulary, which finally becomes reduced to a few prime symbols, and instead relies more and more on the syntax: for in essence this is what abstractism is — the impoverishment of vocabulary and the enrichment of the syntactical relations of expression; in mathematics the vocabulary is reduced to nothing, and the system of expression relies exclusively on the syntax.

In the complicated interplay between vocabulary and syntax, as it appears in the arts, most of the vocables are the result of syntactical combinations which become universally accepted conventions, i.e., as symbols, and as such are regarded as naturalistic representations. We have only to note the stylizations of medieval art which, as the writings of the period advise us, were then considered realistically convincing. That forming of conventional vocables, by which the "content" of the piece of art is transmitted to the spectator, the reader, the listener (procuring for him at the same time the naïve pleasure of recognizing such contents) is the basic characterization of all period styles, style being the fixing of a set of conventions for a certain epoch. Even music, the most "syntactical" of all arts and, therefore, as one would suppose, the most independent of vocable formation, shows in its styles that here, too, the same process of converting syntactical relations into a conventional vocabulary occurs of necessity again and again.

The artist thus graced and cursed with the "style of old age" is not content with the conventional vocabulary provided him by his epoch. For to render the epoch, the whole epoch, he cannot remain within it; he must find a point beyond it. This often appears to him a technical problem, the problem of dissolving the existing vocabulary and, from its syntactical roots, forming his own. His main, sometimes his sole concern is one of craftsmanship: Bach's *Art of the Fugue* was intended as a purely technical work; and the Japanese painter Hokusai, reaching the peak of his mastery at about ninety, had only this to say: "Now at last I begin to learn how one draws a line."

But although the artist's problem seems to be mainly technical, his real impulse goes beyond this — it goes to the universe; and the true piece of art, even though it be the shortest lyric, must always embrace the totality of the world, must be the mirror of that universe, but one of full counterweight. This is felt by every true artist, but is creatively realized only by the artist of old age. The other, who remains bound to his conventional vocabulary, seduced by the known richness of its content — a Frans Hals or a Thomas Wolfe — though he may enlarge his art more and more, reaching a boundless abundance, is never able to achieve his real goal: one cannot capture the universe by snaring its atoms one by one; one can only capture it by showing its basic and essential principles, its basic, and one might even say, its mathematical structure. And here the abstractism of such ultimate principles joins hands with the abstractism of the technical problem: this union constitutes the "style of old age."

The artist who has reached such a point is beyond art. He still produces art, but all the minor and specific problems, with which art in its worldly phase usually deals, have lost interest for him; he is interested neither in the "beauty" of art, nor in the effect which it produces on the public: although more the artist than any other, his attitude approximates that of the scientist, with whom he shares the concern for expressing the universe; however, since he remains an artist, his abstractism is not that of science but — surprisingly enough — very near to that of myth. And there is deep significance in the fact that the creations of the "style of old age" acquire, for the most part, mythical character and even, as in the case of Goethe's *Faust,* have become, being so full of essential symbols, new members of mankind's mythical Pantheon.

BOTH myth and the "style of old age" become abbreviations of the world-content by presenting its structure, and this in its very essence.

"As for myself, I find it difficult to tell all; I am not a God," says Homer. And Rachel Bespaloff adds: "These modest words of Homer could have been adopted by Tolstoy for himself. To both of them it was not necessary to express everything in order to express the Whole. They alone (and, at times, Shakespeare as well) were in possession of those planetarian pauses above the earthly happening, pauses in which history in its continuous flight beyond every human goal reveals its creative un-accomplishment." And in this never-accomplished and always self-creating reality — the building of a new vocabulary out of syntax — lies the essential.

And this explains the connection — at first surprising to us — between myth and mathematics. For every real approach of man to the universe can be called a presentiment of the infinite. Without this, not mathematics, nor myth, nor art, nor any other form of cognition would exist. "The sense of the true is always a kind of conquest, but first it is a gift," says Rachel Bespaloff.

It is this sense of truth, innate in the infinite, which compels man to build perceptive models of the world. For instance, the model of history by Marx employs such economic vocables as exploitation, concentration of capital, etc.; the vocabulary of classical physics consists of certain connotations, such as matter, force, energy, etc.; the psychological model of Freud works with the vocables of drive, suppressed desire, compulsion and the like. In all these models a picture of reality is developed by the composition of the vocables in a syntactical relationship directed by some basic logical rules. In the mythical model these "vocables" consist of the various and imperceptible forces by which primitive man feels himself threatened and moved, within and without; and they are represented by the gods and heroes, their acts and motivations, which then come to form the syntactical texture of the whole model, keeping it in motion. The mythical model is a cosmogony and a theogony ruled by a supreme authority of so remote and abstract a character that even the gods must yield to its commands, becoming merely its actors: this power is Fate. The position of Fate in respect to the mythical model is exactly the same as that of the basic logical rules in respect to the scientific model of the world. No wonder that in the later Greek philosophy Fate and Logos come to have an increasingly identical connotation.

So one returns to Aristotle's remarks on Hesiod, recognizing myth as a kind of pre-science of primitive man, his so-to-speak mathematics. For myth is the first emanation of the Logos in the human mind, in the human language; and never could the human mind or its language have conceived the Logos had not the conception been already formed in the myth. Myth is the archetype of every phenomenal cognition of which the human mind is capable.

Archetype of all human cognition, archetype of science, archetype of art — myth is consequently the archetype of philosophy too. There exists no philosophy which, in its structure and modes of thought, could not be traced back into the parent province of myth. Rachel Bespaloff shows in passing the connection between Platonism and myth; but when in her main argument she interprets Homer's metaphysical standpoint as an identification of Fate and Force —"In the *Iliad* force appears as both the supreme reality and the supreme illusion of life"— she shows implicitly that this blind force, as the nature of nature, as its inescapable law, represents a connection with the metaphysics of existentialism. Philosophy is a constant fight against the remnants of mythical thinking and a constant struggle to achieve mythical structure in a new form, a fight against the metaphysical convention and a struggle to build a new metaphysics; for metaphysics, itself bounded by myth, bounds philosophy, which without these boundaries would have no existence at all. The myth of Jacob who fought against the angel in order to be blessed by him is the myth of philosophy itself.

Myth becomes religion when the mythical model of the universe, hitherto merely cognated or expressed in certain visible forms (of art, etc.) passes into the act of man, coloring his entire behavior, influencing his daily life. In being a member of the *polis* participating in its civic duties, its religious celebrations, its mystery rites, the Greek citizen became a unit in the all-embracing cosmogony (and theogony) which was tentatively limned in his myths. And the medieval peasant, with no knowledge of reading and writing, with no knowledge of the Latin he heard in his church, nevertheless felt himself a part of the Catholic Universe by virtue of the whole hierarchy of values which mirrored the universe, and in which he belonged by living it. The civilization of an epoch is its myth in action.

In other words: civilization, in spite of its practical issues, reveals itself as an all-coordinating myth expressed in a certain vocabulary of human attitudes and actions, which have become conventional and — just for this reason — form a general (and religious) system of values structurally symbolic of the universe. The great periods of culture and their styles, of which the artistic styles are only facets, are marked by the validity of their religious systems of values; they are "closed systems," i.e., systems which cannot be enlarged, but only destroyed and revolutionarily replaced by some other.

When myth through enactment has come to be religion, then art (along with other aspects of existence) becomes of necessity the handmaid of the central religious values, its function being to resymbolize these values which symbolize the world. In this way art is relieved of the labor which otherwise would be required to build its universal structure. It is left free for other tasks, and the human individuality, at first immersed in myth, is now progressively liberated to become the preoccupation of art. The myth of Christ in the art of the Middle Ages is set amidst a landscape of intimate sweetness, of maternal love, of masculine dignity, which embraces the whole scale of human feeling. Thus, after the Dark Ages the rigid grandeur of the myth became increasingly domestic and human, as it was swathed in the charms of legend; for this is the principal means by which it is brought closer to the daily lives of the people. Art, by this means, fulfills its serving task of being educative and social. So in legend the closed system representing the myth reaches a climax of humanization; but it is still a closed system, and for precisely this reason the art of such a period (the fifteenth-century Gothic, for example) renders in full the style of the epoch and in that style, though only in the style, the epoch in its entirety.

THE legend makes myth not only human but humane. Homer, however, although merging the myth with art, does not approach legend but remains austere. Nevertheless his creation is humanization and it begins at the center of the myth with Fate which, according to Rachel Bespaloff (and also to Simone Weil's coincidentally parallel essay[2]), he identifies with Force. Yet this Force, though an anthropomorphic projection of human nature, is far from being humane; nor is Homeric Fate humane. The gods under the spell of such fate are vested with human but not humane qualities.

Indeed, Homer's humanization of the gods goes a step farther. It is true that they are not stripped of their abstract, mythical character; what they were they remain — mere names of the gigantic forces they represent, forces which keep in motion the model of the world and the struggle of man. But by transforming these impersonal qualities, which he leaves to the gods, into an element of poetic irony, Homer achieves their humanization, in a manner specifically his own.

Rachel Bespaloff is probably the first to discover the ironic light which flares up at the collision of the impersonal and the personal (that is, of myth and poetry), a light in which the gods become, as Jean Wahl expresses it, "sometimes slightly less, sometimes slightly more than the human being," so that, on the one side, they are passionately involved in the human struggle, while on the other — and that is especially true of Zeus — they are simply spectators, continuously and almost scientifically detached spectators of the whole human comedy, including even that part they themselves play in it. Against this background of cruel

[2] Broch refers to Simone Weil's essay "The Iliad or the Poem of Force," *Politics*, November 1945, pp. 321–331. — Trans.

abstractness stands the human being: "The heroes of the *Iliad* attain their highest lucidity at a point when justice has been utterly crushed and obliterated."[3]

The constant presence of the divine participants in the *Iliad,* this constant presence of their mythical activity, this constant sense of their remoteness and irony reduces the personal human problem, although potential in the myth, to an ephemeral and — again — nearly abstract role, so that, while it is never lost, it becomes situated at the *soi-distant* periphery of the poem, overshadowed by the terrible Fate of man, by his ultimate realities which are nothing but his longing for life and his certitude of death, both sustained in sorrow. Even the erotic element is removed to this periphery. "Helen," says Rachel Bespaloff, "walks across the *Iliad* as a penitent; misfortune and beauty are consummate in her and lend majesty to her step."

Herein lies the "great style" of the classics, which, while always being tied to the myth of the central value, never loses the flash of irony. As Rachel Bespaloff quotes Nietzsche: "To be a classic, one must have *all* the gifts and *all* the needs, but one must force them all under the same yoke."

THE "great style" of Christian culture was reached in the pre-Renaissance; the time when the mystics opened the path for the Protestant revolution.

The Protestant revolution was one against the hierarchical concept of myth. As a Christian, man was still enacting this myth. But he had also discovered that this myth he must enact was none other than the creation of his own mind, a creation that God, by a direct act of grace, had imbedded in his soul. With this discovery man could renounce the outside hierarchy, for he was building up the universe within.

[3.] Jean André Wahl (1888–1974), French philosopher, professor at the Sorbonne, was known for his studies of Descartes, Hegel, Kierkegaard, and Heidegger. Broch did not give the source of the quote. — Trans.

On this basic change of view the human personality as such attained new status. Heretofore it could be used only as an illustration of the myth itself — as legend. Now it was drawn from the periphery and, residing in the center, shaped about itself a humanistic world.

And this casts a new light on the phenomenon of the "great style" in the arts. The great style comes into being when the crust of the closed system cracks open to give birth to a new system. At this moment, when there is still vitality and security in the old system and its forms, still certitude in the myth, the new system, vitalized by hope and striving toward openness, creates its own new form — the great style. This is to be seen in Michelangelo, in the Greek cycle of Aeschylus, or in the sculptures of Olympia, works which, as Rachel Bespaloff points out, share the gravity of Homer.

The "great style" is security and revolution in one, and it lasts only as long as the revolutionary tendency is aflame, but is doomed to harden once more into a system, closed as was its predecessor.

The Protestant epoch — the Protestant universe — had its "great style" as well, actually one of the greatest in all history, that of the Dutch school in painting, of Bach and his predecessors in music, of Milton in poetry, and finally of Kant in philosophy, where we find less a style than the building of a Protestant scholasticism. And here, as before, the "great style" signalized the end of its epoch, when the now closed system of Protestantism had to be reopened by a new revolutionary act.

This verified the prophecy of Catholicism: in the eyes of the Church the Protestant revolt had been the first step in the destruction of the Western Christian unity, the first step in the heretical secularization of the human mind; and so it proved. In an irrevocable process, lasting from the eighteenth to the twentieth century, the Western structure of values lost its Christian center.

These one hundred and fifty years of disintegration have produced a certain attitude in man which is called romanticism. As long as the system of values is fully alive and its universe intact, man is able to solve his private and personal problems within the existing framework, while in times of disintegration such solution is achieved only when the universe is shaped anew for (and from) every particular case. It is precisely this necessity of building the universe up from every single case, and of course from each human soul, that is the basic characteristic of romanticism. Obviously this romantic procedure could never have come to pass without the preparation of Protestantism, by the tenets of which man's soul is linked directly with the universe and with God.

The Protestant dogma gives the human soul a far greater autonomy than does Catholicism, and in romanticism this autonomy becomes absolute. It is for this reason that romantic art, even when produced by a great artist, can no longer achieve the "great style," which always requires the validity of a universally accepted myth. For whatever universe may be built from the single instance, its validity is limited by the boundaries of the autonomous human soul; though it may be approved by a certain number of people, its general, not to speak of its eternal, validity remains insecure. Infected by this ultimate insecurity, the romantic artist acquires the characteristic attitude of longing, longing in particular for the religious unity of the past. Thus wishing to solve his problems in an absolute way, and feeling that Protestantism is largely responsible for the dangers of his situation, the romantic in his homesickness is led back to Catholicism, to find shelter in the Church.

Every true artist, aware that he must form his own universe, is in some ways a rebel, willing to shatter the closed system into which he is born. But he should realize that revolution is not enough, that he must also build anew the essential framework of the world. And just that is achieved by the style of old age; for this style, revolutionary by means of its abstractness, gains a level one can only call the super-religious. On this level stands Bach in his last works, Goethe and Beethoven as well, though they, born in a period when the religious system of values was already dissolved, had to reach the abstract by the detour of romanticism.

In moving from romanticism to the abstract they were precursors; Tolstoy was no less a precursor, even a more radical one. *War and Peace,* though it cannot be called a work of old age, clearly has left romanticism behind, anticipating the style of old age in a new and abstract model of the universe — an Homeric universe as Rachel Bespaloff has rightly discovered. But Tolstoy's radicalism did not content itself with this artistic approach to myth; in contrast to Goethe and Beethoven, who were, in spite of their human greatness, preponderantly artists, Tolstoy was striving for more: he was striving for the complete abstractism of a new theogony. For the style of old age, which in time he achieved, had another goal than the Homeric one, a goal nearer to Hesiod and Solon than to Homer, and the merging of myth and art; with a zeal akin to that of Savonarola, he aspired to radical finalities, and so withdrew from art altogether to construct his own ethical universe.

In the case of Beethoven and Goethe it was not only their personal genius (as in Bach's case) which compelled them toward a new style, they were enjoined to it by their epoch, in which the closed values were already being shattered. There is a fair possibility that Homer, too, felt some such command from his epoch. Cretan civilization, we know, was a late and mature one. The Geometric vases of its early period hint at a closed system, religious in nature — a medieval hierarchy of values. But the "Saffron Gatherer" of the eighteenth century B.C. already indicates the free naturalistic culture of a ripening age, characterized by the liberation of human personality, and the following period is that of the luxurious palace of Knossos, contemporaneous with the romantic mysticism of Ikhnaton's Egypt. The Eastern Mediterranean was bound in a network of commerce and trade: it was as much an age of aesthetic sophistication and of the personal problem as the later Roman period. Late Minoan art shows refined types of a highly developed court civilization — was not Trojan Paris one of them?—and bears indubitable marks of a romantic period in which the beginning of the end shows its first symptoms.

The realization of this tragic situation came with the onslaught of the Achaians. If the *Iliad* be basically Cretan in origin, it is from this dread encounter that it received its mythical shape. It is specifically mythical that the two types of the old and the new, Paris and Hector, the one a playboy and the other a patriot, should be presented as coeval and brothers. Hector, "man and among men a prince," is subject to the apocalyptic mood of his time and, therefore, affectionately recognizes the peaceful achievements of the civilization for which he is ready to fight and to die. As later in Tolstoy, the personal problems fade away, and in the rising contours of the new myth the human element is reduced to sorrow and mourning, both sober and unromantic, but great as Fate itself.

It is unlikely that Homer was Cretan; the surge of the poem is Achaian: its impact is the same as that of the first Greek carvings, not at all like those of the late Cretan period. However, it is unimaginable without the Cretan influence: were the sources of the poem purely Greek, it would exult far more than it does in the Grecian victory; only Cretan influence makes Homer's impartiality credible, an impartiality which diminishes his joy for the Greeks and balances it by his lament for the Trojans. "Call him Achilles or Hector, the conqueror is like all conquerors, and the conquered like all the conquered." Moreover, this impartiality is an aesthetic one not only on the part of the gods (whose impartiality is not justice), or on the part of the poet, but on that of his characters as well. Rachel Bespaloff, in one of her most impressive passages, interprets the meeting of Priam and Achilles who achieve a moment of kinship through their mutual recognition of each other's beauty. And let us not forget that it was beauty, Helen's beauty, which gave life to the whole conflict.

This exaltation of the aesthetic, doubtless of Cretan origin, and originally strange to the barbarian Greeks, took a marvelous hold on them. In an astonishingly short time, they wrought from it a new and Hellenic form. Out of the broken fragments of the Cretan world was developed the poetic myth which became the religion and life of the Greek world.

Whether Homer existed or not, he is described as a very old man, blind as Milton, blind as Bach, blind as Fate; the style of old age in all its greatness, coolness, and abstract transparency is so obvious in his work that people had necessarily to conceive him in this form. He himself became myth, and since behind almost every myth stands some historical reality, we ought not to ask whether he existed or not, but should simply accept him as the mythical old man, the eternal paradigm of an epoch which demands the rebirth of myth.

It is somehow a blasphemy to compare our time with that of the Homeric epics; it is blasphemy because it was the fantasy of the Nazis to become the new Achaians demolishing an old civilization. However, it is not necessary to compare Hitler with Achilles when we compare the Mycenian cultural crisis with our own.

It need not be stressed again that, owing to its loss of religious centrality, the present world, at least of the West (although the East surely has not remained untouched), has entered a state of complete disintegration of values, a state in which each single value is in conflict with every other one, trying to dominate them all. The apocalyptic events of the last decades are nothing but the unavoidable outcome of such a dissolution.

Along with these developments, the romantic uneasiness was constantly on the increase. Seeking in an empirical period for some validity, romanticism could only join with an empirical science in a progression which (splitting the world more and more into fragmentary disciplines) increased the hunger of its search. Art became naturalistic, veristic, scientific in its methods, running through the sequences of Impressionism, until at last, in an ultimate despair of expression, it has become expressionistic. If in all these forms it renders the reality of our time, it does so in fact only as anarchy reflecting anarchy.

Thus it is only natural that there came to be a mood of deep distaste for this kind of art, and even for art at all. This distaste is felt neither by the general public which, though sometimes bored, consumes what it is served, nor is it felt by the pseudo-artist who accepts success as a proof of his quality, but it is felt by the few genuine artists, and by those who know that art which does not render the totality of the world is no art. If art can or may exist further, it has to set itself the task of striving for the essential, of becoming a counterbalance to the hypertrophic calamity of the world. And imposing such a task on the arts, this epoch of disintegration imposes on them the style of old age, the style of the essential, the style of the abstract.

The French painters at the turn of the century were the first — significantly guided by technical considerations — who were aware that the whole naturalistic, and unavoidably naturalistic, vocabulary had become obsolete, and that the essential had to be found, even at the price of abstractness. More and more the painter lost interest in the individual fact; the artist's goal was no longer to reproduce the smiling Mrs. X, but (whether or not he achieved it) to strive for the essence of smile. This search led, through increasing sophistications of technique, to the experiments of non-objective art.

Picasso's development is paradigmatic of these processes, all the more so since he achieved in one work a real and perhaps the first full expression of our time: this is *Guernica*, a picture so abstract that it could even renounce all color, a picture expressing horror, sorrow, mourning — nothing else, and for this very reason the strongest rebellion against the evil.

Seen from the technical side, abstract art deals with problems very near to those of music, for music is the abstract art *par excellence.* The further the arts move in the direction of abstractism, the closer become the theoretical ties between them: the connection between music and painting is stronger in our time than ever before. And this applies even to poetry and literature; the work of Joyce gains its artistic validity in a very large measure from the musical elements and principles on which it is built.

The striking relationship between the arts on the basis of their common abstractism, their common style of old age, this hallmark of our epoch is the cause of the inner relationship between artists like Picasso, Stravinsky and Joyce. This relationship is not only striking in itself but also by reason of the parallelism through which the style of old age was imposed on these men, even in their rather early years.

Nevertheless, abstractism forms no *Gesamtkunstwerk* — the ideal of the late romantic; the arts remain separate. Literature especially can never become completely abstract and "musicalized": therefore the style of old age relies here much more on another symptomatic attitude, namely on the trend toward myth. It is highly significant that Joyce goes back to the *Odyssey*. And although this return to myth — already anticipated in Wagner — is nowhere so elaborated as in Joyce's work, it is for all that a general attitude of modern literature: the revival of Biblical themes, as, for instance, in the novels of Thomas Mann, is an evidence of the impetuosity with which myth surges to the forefront of poetry. However, this is only a return — a return to myth in its ancient forms (even when they are so modernized as in Joyce), and so far it is not a new myth, not *the* new myth. Yet, we may assume that at least the first realization of such a new myth is already evident, namely in Franz Kafka's writings.

In Joyce one may still detect neo-romantic trends, a concern with the complications of the human soul, which derives directly from nineteenth-century literature, from Stendhal, and even from Ibsen. Nothing of this kind can be said about Kafka. Here the personal problem no longer exists, and what seems still personal is, in the very moment it is uttered, dissolved in a super-personal atmosphere. The prophecy of myth is suddenly at hand. And like every true prophecy it is ethical: for where now are the old problems of poetry, the problems of love, marriage, betrayal and jealousy, when murder and rape and degradation are threatening the human being at every moment of his life, and nothing remains but sorrow and mourning? And what painter would still invite the spectator to rest under the idyllic trees of his landscape, when the landscapes of this earth have become exclusively roads of flight and persecution? Abstractism had attacked the private problems of men from the technical side, eliminating them from the realm of art; with Kafka it becomes apparent that they have lost their ethical validity as well: private problems have become as distasteful as sordid crimes. It is the last condemnation of all romanticism, of all these direct connections between the single private case and the universe, between the single fact and the general idea, as it is overemphasized by the romantic conception.

However, near as this point of view is to that of the French existentialists, Kafka does not belong to them, and his distaste for the private problem, especially in art, is not identical with their "nausée," though like them he knows that the utter isolation in which the single fact is plunged reduces all art and literature to non-existence. For they still remain in the sphere of traditional literature, traditional even when no longer employed for its own sake, but only, as in the existentialist novels and plays, for its value as parable — often approaching legend — to illustrate and concretize their philosophical theories; while Kafka aims in the exactly opposite direction, namely at abstraction, not at concretization — at an untheoretical abstraction to which he was driven exclusively by ethical concerns — and therefore transcends literature. He has reached the point of the Either-Or: either poetry is able to proceed to myth, or it goes bankrupt. Kafka, in his presentiment of the new cosmogony, the new theogony that he had to achieve, struggling with his love for literature, his disgust for literature, feeling the ultimate insufficiency of any artistic approach, decided (as did Tolstoy, faced with a similar decision) to quit the realm of literature, and asked that his work be destroyed; he asked this for the sake of the universe whose new mythical concept had been bestowed upon him.

MAN as such is our time's problem; the problems of men are fading away and are even forbidden, morally forbidden. The personal problem of the individual has become a subject of laughter for the gods, and they are right in their lack of pity. The individual is reduced to nothing, but humanity can stand against the gods and even against Fate.

This is the dynamic of the Homeric myth. And as a phenomenon of far-reaching importance, it reappears instinctively in the arts of our time. It is like a foreplan of the new myth which in the future may stand at the religious center of mankind's system of values. Art of itself cannot form the myth, but it points in that direction, because it is expression of the human needs.

Hitler thought to establish the new myth by forbidding the personal problems of men to exist. But his was pseudo-myth, for the real myth lives in the problem of human existence, the problem of man as such. However, if God has to exist, the devil eventually has to serve Him, and it is just the Nazi terror which may still ripen humanity for the ethical theogony in which the new myth will receive its being: if this happens, Fate again will be humanized, and presumably it will be not only human, as was Homer's Force, but also humane, in so far as it is in accord with Europe's Christian tradition. Homer's Force was to have been supplanted by Jehovah's justice, Jehovah's justice by Christ's love. "Through cruelty force confesses its powerlessness to achieve omnipotence."

To show these correspondences seems to have been Rachel Bespaloff's purpose in linking the Homeric epic with Biblical prophecy. In doing so she endows the Homeric work with a new significance for our time — a significance rather Kierkegaardian than existentialist — and it is from here that her interpretation gains a large measure of its essential importance. Were this the only justification of her analysis, this alone would suffice.

Some Comments on the Philosophy and Technique of Translating *(1946)*[1]

translated by John Hargraves

To PUT it directly at the outset: Nothing in life is accomplished without intuition, and without the love of one's work. Whether it is a translation, a good shot at billiards, or whatever it may be, we know little of the reasons that make something work. "It just happened to be."[2] No billiards player can work out the mathematical and physical equations that control how he directs the balls, and when asked how he could do so, he will murmur something like accident, mystery, or intuition; if he realizes that such banalities really are no explanation at all, he may simply shrug his shoulders.

I did not come here to shrug my shoulders for you, nor would I like to come up with trivial and banal explanations. I simply want to tell you

---

[1] Hermann Broch, "Einige Bemerkungen zur Philosophie und Technik des Übersetzens," *Schriften zur Literatur 2: Theorie* (Frankfurt am Main: Suhrkamp, 1975), pp. 61–86.

[2] Broch wrote this sentence in English, doubtless meaning, "It just happened."

some of my experiences in translating *The Death of Virgil* and give you some of the ideas that came out of this, particularly from conversations with its author, Hermann Broch.[3] You will perhaps believe me when I say that this job was so difficult that it left me little time to consider the mysterious and intuitive impulses behind it. And yet, the topic I shall begin with is not just a mystery, but a double mystery.

In short, I think I should begin with the mystery of human nature, for every problem in the end leads to this mystery, not least the problem of translation and translatability. Everything that bears the mark of humankind has at its deepest level a general structural uniformity (which it is the translator's job to know, given his eminently democratic and pacifist mission), and were it not for this structural uniformity in every expressive gesture of humanity, then there could truly be no translatability. The necessary third component *(tertium comparationis)* for all translation is Man himself, and the uniform basic structure of the mystery called the human spirit.

What is this uniformity manifested in? The human spirit as such cannot be seen; its existence is perceived only through its expressions, its projections into the external world. These are rendered only through the matter of that external world, and so they are merely symbols for what is to be expressed. Tears themselves are just a symbol of pain, not the pain itself; a smile is just the symbol of the joy that moves the soul in its invisible depths. Put differently, even the most basic emotions like pain and joy, grief and pleasure are only seen through symbols. Although the physical gestures in which they are expressed are, so to speak, natural symbols, animal-like in their natural directness, there are other symbols with which man expresses himself and his reactions to the world, his inner and outer reality, symbols less animal-like, but no less natural. For example, the rhythmic ornaments that the savage carves onto his clay pots, his images of human and animal forms, are just as natural an

[3.] Broch wrote this essay for his translator, Jean Starr Untermeyer, whom he wanted to read this essay at Yale as her own. She refused.

expression of his physicality as gestures, words, dances, and songs: These are the outlet of his physicality, the way he symbolizes his world and his own existence. There is no such thing as an unnatural symbol. For man's nature is his culture, which is nothing other than the ability to use symbolic language, the universal language of symbols, manifest in every culture. And no matter how differently or highly developed it may be, a culture will always have that kernel of naturalness inside; the only thing unnatural, counter to nature, is a regression to earlier forms of symbols. This is the great mystery of human nature: man's capacity for culture, that he can and must build culture with symbols. And if I say this is a double mystery, despite its uniformity, I do so because of another type of uniformity — every symbol is both content and form, that is, its purpose is to express something specific, but it can only do this when the material in which it expresses itself is given a specific form.

But what is meant by this mysterious uniformity, which itself holds a mystery within it? A phenomenon has uniformity only when that phenomenon exhibits constant qualities independent of time and space. This would mean that every human expression must exhibit some kind of constancy with regard to content and form, in its use as a symbol. Which immediately leads to the question: What would such constancy look like? It is certainly conceivable that the myriad diverse contents of human expression could fall under a uniform constant principle of *form,* but can there be a constant principle of *content* itself, without radically changing the concept of content, which after all is totally based on diversity? Would this not completely annul the idea of content? In other words, it is certainly conceivable that all symbols are formed according to certain constant formal laws and that the contents of all symbols depend on these laws, but the reverse, namely, constancy of contents, seems almost absurd (and I emphasize "seems"). With the highly paradigmatic case of language, it is quite conceivable that there is a constant principle of form for everything that the human tongue can utter; to go even further, it is quite likely that language possesses a general, uniform meta-syntax. But it seems at first impossible to propose the same rule for the actual contents of speech, since sounds in combination, understood as words and thus supposedly symbolizing contents, apparently are produced in total freedom, arbitrarily, and without restriction.

Nonetheless, in the realm of nature there is neither freedom nor arbitrariness, and even if the growth and richness of expressive symbols have come about naturally, as we maintain, there is still doubtless a natural selection among these supposedly arbitrary symbols, eliminating all those not appropriate to the natural growth of the respective symbolic language. This would happen whether the symbols were words, material images, sounds, or merely gestures. But selection only occurs when something is present. Nature is a whole, every organism is a whole, and it is the organism as a whole that rejects anything unsuited to it. The same is true of the symbols human beings create and use; each of the different symbol-languages forms an organic whole, and these also in combination will form superordinated organic complexes such as language families, etc., perhaps even entire classes of expression, in which the whole entity is continually deciding on the acceptability of a vocabulary unit (and so not just linguistic ones). So those expressive units allowed by the system all have an internal, symbol-content relationship to one another, for selection implies relationship. A small example to illustrate this point: Man is continually subject to basic sensations like pain and pleasure; they accompany everything he feels and says; this being the case, every one of his higher symbols must contain something of these primal symbols; everything expressing pain must show, as it were, the shimmer of a "primal tear," and in everything reflecting joy a smile is somehow perceptible. The constant connection of all human symbols to these primal emotions and symbols makes clear a basic pattern: All human symbols fit into a comprehensive relationship naturally determined by their content. They continually influence each other in their formation, give each other meaning and content, set up hierarchies, differentiate themselves, while at the same time simplifying themselves, since the process necessarily standardizes things into groups. A simplifying, ordering principle is based on content, and while this principle obviously can apply to form as well, we may still properly speak (despite our earlier statement) of a uniformity of content.

Now for the other side of the question, for every organism of symbols, no matter what its area of reference, is also a system. That is, its parts are related not just by the contents characteristic of that particular group, their connection is not just the reciprocal or formative influence they have on their respective contents: Rather, the parts are a system of formal relationships, exactly the type of system one thinks of *a priori* as uniform and constant. This systemic relationship assigns parts their place in the whole, regulates their reciprocal functions, and thus collectively drives the function of the entire organism. To use our earlier example: The inner relationship of vocabulary units, their mutual structural dependence on content, assures the organic character of a language but does not make it usable, or even speakable: This is possible only with the appropriate syntax. Only through the formal rules of syntax is a word transformed into part of a sentence. Only in a context that is logical, dynamic, and formal does a word acquire its actual meaning; only then is meaningful speech possible. This is even clearer in the case of musical language: The vocabulary units of music, tones, in themselves have minimal meaning content, even if they have specific and undeniably natural relationships to one another, as shown by their different harmonic keys. But it is only through musical syntax, only through a logical architecture, of which these tones are the building blocks, that a form based on tones (as opposed to form based on content, as above) becomes a content based on form, or meaningful music.

So I distinguish between form based on content, and content based on form. But are these two completely separate things? To keep to our example, is one the domain of verbal language, the other of musical language? By no means. One need only think of setting words to music to see how much the two processes enhance one another. Music can translate the spoken word into its own language, can at the same time so heighten it and deepen it, as to make the word almost vanish as a straightforward vocabulary unit containing meaning. What is left is its content as pure sense, wholly subsumed, wholly absorbed by musical form, musical syntax, finding in this very dissolution its lasting meaning and preservation (I think here of the double meaning of Hegel's *aufgehoben,* destruction and preservation at once). Something similar happens with gesture, which through music and in music becomes dance.

The converse is not true: Music can hardly be translated into words, and, except for the conductor's vocabulary of gestures, only a fractional part of music can be represented by the gestures of dance. The fact that this is so indicates that the number and variety of syntactically formed contents, that is, those contents based on form, such as in music, have always to be greater numerically than the wealth of forms based on content, just as the theoretically infinite variables of mathematics will always exceed those of objects in the real world, and certainly that of words (not to mention the even more limited diversity of gestures), which portray only a small selection of possible combinations of things of this world. As long as its symbolic value is alive, a single creation of words, or of any symbolic language, can evoke an innumerable variety of musical settings; as long as Catholics believe, the rites and liturgy of the Mass will be set and reset to music.

A symbol that is alive is a symbol that is understood; with the problem of understanding, the problem of communicating, we touch the problem of translation. When does the *content* of a symbol retain such lively interest to the mind that it can count on finding ever new musical settings? And even given a symbol's currency, why is it, given the abundance of contents that music has formed or could form, that appropriate musical settings for that symbol can always be found? These two questions are obviously as connected as form is to content, and the understanding on which both depend is itself clearly dependent on a third term of comparison, one that can act as a constant for both formal and contentual aspects of the questions. This was my reason for indicating at the start that the third component necessary for translation is to be found in the uniform and constant nature of the human spirit. And in fact, when we search for symbols that are consistent over time, we find mostly those by means of which man represents his inner and outer reality most simply and comprehensively: All primal myths belong to these fundamental symbols of humanity as a whole, as do all religious rituals, insofar as they have evolved naturally, and thus have been influenced by myth. It need not be further explained that the Catholic Mass with its word and gesture belongs here as well. But keep in mind that we are dealing here exclusively with form based on content, and that both myth and ritual have a need for musical emphasis, musical presentation — for music completes them. Music, too, strives to present a total view of man, doing so chiefly through content based on form, for herein lies its syntactic, one could even say abstract, essence, and not in form based on content. Music does this not only in its entirety, but in each of its works, provided they are truly musical; music depicts syntactically the essence of all the abstract logical qualities through which man understands himself and his world. And the more acutely man develops abstract logical and mathematical abilities to understand his world (in this the West is ahead of the East, at least at present), the more music and the form-derived contents of music will become the total symbol of his innermost logical structure.

It seems to me that much in the development of Western art, and music's striking importance in it, can be explained from this point of view. But I mean this just as an example, and not to suggest a norm; art can and will continue to develop along completely different ways. Nor have I dared push this hypothesis so far for its own sake; rather, I was drawn to it because it reveals a very plausible set of facts: that man always endeavors to portray himself and his innermost structure through symbols, that he does this with the materials available to him, the things of real life, and that this symbolization, like the structure of

the human spirit as such, consists of content and form, of content-based
form and form-based content, and, moreover, to demonstrate the permanent validity of their most basic manifestations. The basic manifestations of all symbols are Archetype and Logos: content in the Archetype,
as uncovered by Jung in myths, and form in the Logos, whose endless
discovery and rediscovery is the subject of all philosophy, and not just
Platonic philosophy. Whatever symbols man uses to express himself,
these symbols are inevitably steeped in archetype and the Logos, whose
indissoluble bond defines the basic structure of the symbol. Thus the
symbol also reflects the basic structure of the human spirit, the human
soul, and in this way becomes the means, the sole means, of understanding from one person to another. For in every true symbol, man sees himself, and finding himself in it, seeing himself reflected in it, he understands that symbol. This is nowhere so evident as in the major symbol
groups that art uses to represent itself; for even though the symbol's
structure is present in all human expression, in art self-representation is
the real end in itself, its reason for being, and therein is its legitimation.

Whether the chicken or the egg came first is an idle question, and it is
just as idle to ask whether Logos precedes Archetype. They are inevitably bound together, and because they reflect the basic structure of our
human existence in this bond, we can bring intellectual understanding
and aesthetic appreciation to otherwise totally alien symbolic expressions of other cultures, even to the domestic and artistic products of
primitive civilizations, however far removed by space or time. Only
because of this can we grasp emotionally and intellectually the Egyptian
language of forms, be it that of pre-Pharaonic times 5,000 years ago, or
the late Alexandrian period; or that of the Aztec and Inca empires, or of
ancient China or India. They all of them are part of our own existence.
We find in them those primal symbols that live in us, we find the un-
changing problems of form with which the present-day artist must
struggle, even if he never reaches the simple, stark solutions of the
mythic age. Through all different conditions and stages of development

we find the same rules for linking the vocabulary of symbols together, the same logical syntactic structure. All of this is in all of us, and because it is, we can translate. The mystery of translatability is the mystery of our own existence.

God has equipped the human race with 72 different language groups — Prof. Weigand[4] probably knows this better than anyone — but since the 72 original nations, in accordance with the will of God, all sprang from Adam's seed, their languages were all mutually translatable, or at least up until the translation catastrophe of the Tower of Babel. This, too, supports our theory of translatability, which derives from the existence of man, of Adam, as such, and if we accept this, then this theory of translatability will doubtless prove true as well for the act of translation, and even for the technique of translation.

Translations are not musical settings, but likewise work in the realm of expression and symbol, namely, language. The common denominator of two languages, their translation denominator, so to speak, is thus certainly greater than that of language and music. But this denominator depends on the Logos, and nowhere is the effect of Logos clearer than in language, for through that medium Logos expresses the logical coherence of the external world, that is, causality. All that is rational and logical in one's understanding of the world is manifest in language, even logic itself (though it can also be written in mathematical signs). And logic in particular points out that all language structure is based on a meta-syntax, regardless of the various grammars in which it is concretely expressed. Even where a language is not constructed on the Indo-European model of subject-predicate-object, even where it does not project an acting subject in relations with things and expressions (note the anthropomorphic nature of this last statement, in which language makes projections as if it were a person), even in those languages

---

4. Hermann J. Weigand (1892–1985), American Germanist Emeritus at Yale. Weigand had invited Broch and his translator, Jean Starr Untermeyer, to speak to the Germanic Club at Yale in 1946. — Trans.

that see the causality of the world less as anthropomorphic and dynamic, and rather as more static and final, more pictorially, even in those languages there still appear the meta-syntactic relations of the general and the specific, of cause and effect. If God had confined Himself to the principles of Logos and logical syntax in the creating of language (and at an early moment of Creation, it looked as though He meant to), if He had not reserved archetypes as principles of individuation (for emergencies like Babel), He would "logically" have ended up with a single unitary language, rather than 72 different language types. This unitary language would have been manifest as content based on form, in the manner of mathematical language, and not as form based on content, like concrete languages. Babel notwithstanding, the unitary form of languages has been maintained in the formative principle of meta-syntax, and its preservation can be seen as God's grace as well as curse: Because of it, we can translate from language to language.

If I set up the principle of individuation (i.e., archetypes) as the opposite of a principle of syntactic uniformity, I certainly do not mean that the various languages result from the breakup of humanity's common mythology into 72 national mythologies. To be sure, the national mythology of a people is somehow connected to the forming of its language, but it would be hard to get beyond this "somehow" without falling back onto questionable, hard-to-prove hypotheses. I mean, rather, that every symbolic language, and certainly every national word-language, forms an organic whole, whose parts, namely, word-symbols, have an archetypal relationship. This archetypal relationship gives each language's syntax its particular tone, the coloration that distinguishes one grammar from another. It is an archetypal relationship and an archetypal coloration, because it remains constant for every language, that is, accompanies it through its whole evolution. Commonly called the "spirit" of a language, it cannot be understood with dictionaries and grammar-book learning, and it plays a dominant role in the work of translation.

So translation takes place between two language organisms that possess certain similarities of structure in syntax but differ so much from each other with respect to types, to archetypes, that for expressions to be understood in both, the need for translation arises. Their syntactic conformity makes the translation easier, but it would be wrong to assume that related vocabularies ease the job in a similar way. One thinks for example of two dialects of German, a language rich in dialects; it is technically possible, of course, to translate a North German *Plattdeutsch* text, say, of Fritz Reuter, into Viennese without further ado, but the result would seem strange, even grotesque. The reason for this may be found in the following: In every language organism, there is an untranslatable core, peculiar to that language alone, whose untranslatability is based on regional and sometimes even local bonds, and the more closely the two language organisms are related, the larger that part of their mutual association that is taken up by that untranslatable core. Thus, two kinds of language prove to be especially suited to translation: first, those where the target language is so removed from the source language in time or place that the original regional coloration is meaningless; and second, those that have already shed their regional character and become national written languages. Of course, the same also applies to some extent to the target language; it is easier to translate into a neutral written language than into a local dialect. Though this is certainly not the only reason for the great traffic in translation that started in Europe with the Renaissance (this came from a whole series of other, in many ways more important, motives, which were all interconnected, from the religious turmoil of the Reformation to the invention of printing), it should not be forgotten that this also was the period when written language was being formed and stabilized. The creation of the German written language went hand in hand with Luther's translation of the Bible.

So translation means opposing one language to another, and doing justice to both. A translator working just with dictionaries and grammars will not gain access to this level of translation. So, must the translator rely totally on his linguistic intuition, by virtue of which he comprehends both languages in their entirety? No, this would be pretentious; one need not resort to such irrational requirements. Even recognizing all the irrational and intuitive elements of language, it is quite rational to require that a translator understand the language from which he is translating well enough to grasp the meaning of its statements. For that is what he should translate: not words and sentences, but their meaning. Once he understands the sentence to be translated, his job is to express it in the target language, in which he must be completely at home. He expresses this sense in the target language as if there were no original before him. If he succeeds in this, and then compares the resulting sentence with the original, he will usually notice, to his surprise, that the syntactic peculiarities of the original appear again in the target language, transformed appropriately, true to the original. For this he must give credit to that common meta-syntax that operates inside and behind both languages. The precondition of such a pleasant surprise is, of course, that the original sentence reflects its own language organism faultlessly.

Let me explain with an example[5] from my own translation. Broch's sentences in *The Death of Virgil* are extraordinary for their unusual length. The reasons for this I need not explain or defend here, but I should like to call your attention to the peculiar floating rhythm of this example:

German example

And here you have the translation:

Translation

I hope you would grant that my translation has the qualities of English, i.e., that it is constructed in the spirit of English and so it fits organically into that language. Nonetheless, or perhaps for just that

[5.] Broch never specified which passages he meant.

reason, it has a rhythm that is highly similar, I hope, to that of the original. Had I taken the reverse tack and simply tried to imitate slavishly in English the composition and rhythm of Broch's sentence, I would have created a monster and a corruption of the original sense.

During my work many people advised me simply to break up Broch's sentences in English, because long sentences were "not English." This remained a problem for me until I discovered that the English language can easily accommodate long sentences, and that the assertion that long sentences are "un-English" is a highly superficial judgment. Going beneath the superficial, we find something quite different: namely, a basic difference in the way English and German sentences are built. German sentences have a periodic, hierarchical construction: The main clause should contain the essential, and where possible, new information for the reader; everything else is assigned to dependent clauses, so that descriptors of a person or thing are in an attributive clause, especially when these attributes are already known. The situation is similar with any ancillary descriptions of real or imagined situations: An entire architecture of super- and subordinated clauses is intertwined around the main clause, and to clarify their logical connection, a large number of conjunctions are employed, such as "so," "consequently," "because," "whereas," "however," etc. One could call this periodic structure pedagogic or pedantic, particularly when compared with the French, but one must also admit this logical architecture has a peculiar beauty whose charms are hard to resist once one has gotten used to it. But it is just this that English speakers find difficult, for the idiom of English does not care much about whether information is super- or subordinate, whether modifiers for persons or things have been mentioned earlier or not. English does not hesitate to repeat such things if need be, even in a main clause, and it just sets out what it has to say sequentially, without bothering to interject clarifying conjunctions. So the reader is not presented the information in its complete logical construct; this is left more to his imagination and powers of association, his free grasp of things, thus showing the reader a larger measure of trust than, say, German would. For a quick mind, epigrammatic hints are sufficient, and this is in fact the route that English style has taken since the mid-nineteenth century, and even if this were largely attributable to the influence of English journalese, this would not quite amount to a decline of style. However, it would be real intellectual decline if the reason were sheer convenience, if English speakers were to refuse every complex idea *a priori* if expressing it required a long sentence, or, if complexity were inevitable, they were to chop those ideas up into short sentences. No, the English language not only allows, it actually requires long sentences in certain intellectual constructs; it just wants them laid out according to its own rules.

I have never translated sentences, just ideas and what they mean. So where my sentences are as long as those of the original, I believe I can say that this proves their structure is right. If in some (albeit rare) instances shorter sentence forms have resulted, I believe usually the same thing could have been done with the original. Allow me to give an example of such a long sentence:

German example

And here the translation:

Translation

If you compare the original sentence with the translation, you will notice many considerable deviations in structural details: In general they are almost always the result of the English requirement for directness; the German "packeted" sentence has been mostly avoided, I hope, as has the accumulation of conjunctions that stud the German sentence.

If we pursue the reason for all these syntactic differences, we begin to suspect that German and English, despite their close relationship, have developed into two different types of language. It is as if an English statement were centered more on fact, and therefore on words, while the German seems to be based almost completely on the relationship between facts, on the syntactic interconnection of its words. This is supported by the fact that English has almost four times as many words as German, a ratio even more striking when one looks at the number of nouns in each language. The fact that German makes up for its lack of words by turning its verbs and adjectives into nouns, and that new noun-combinations *(Substantivkomposita)* can be formed *ad hoc* all the time, only reinforces our point, for this all shows how a syntactically oriented language by using its own peculiar syntax can intervene in the formation of content, that is, of vocabulary. In short, from this simplified viewpoint English is a word-language and German is a sentence-language, so that in German content based on form predominates, and in English, form based on content. An extreme stylist in German, and here I am thinking more of Thomas Mann than of Broch, would arrive at extraordinary sentence constructions, while in English a Joyce has become an architect of words.

Simplification has its faults. Therefore if we were to generalize this idea of the two language types, and categorize the Indo-European languages this way, grouping Greek and German with the sentence-languages, and Latin and its derivatives with the word-languages (the specific word orientation of English thus coming from its Latin-French admixture), we would soon be mired in contradictions. Certainly, the Latin spirit was once decidedly more factual than the Greek, while the fact remains that, relatively speaking, the vocabulary of Latin was quite small, and that even today French's vocabulary is substantially smaller than German's. Moreover (one must almost say consequently), neither Latin nor French is by any means as word-oriented as one might assume from this; on the contrary, their mode of expression is based emphatically on syntax, even if it has a different coloration from German.

One is on very thin ice with all this, and the layman in particular should refrain from making such risky typological generalizations. For this reason I have not said that English and German belong to two different language types, but that they have developed this way, regardless of whether there are others of this type or not.

It is also unimportant for the translator whether the two language types his work is concerned with belong to higher typological groups or not. He is interested solely in the two types as such with which he is working, and these he tries to know as thoroughly as possible. And if he is translating from German to English, he cannot avoid taking note of the differences between word- and sentence-languages, between content-based form and form-based content, and to direct his work accordingly. There is no translator of German who has not been tripped up by its substantives made from verbs and adjectives, or who did not get headaches from all its composite words with their tricky double or multiple meanings. What is the translator to do with a word like *"verwandlungsstark"* (transformation-strong)? Is the meaning here that something has gained strength *(Stärke)* through transformation *(Verwandlung)?* Or that a particularly powerful transformation has taken place? Or a strong potential for transformation? A German would generally answer that this would be evident from the context, but on analyzing it with this in mind, one usually finds, surprisingly, that all the various meanings fit the context equally: Indeed, it was precisely for the sake of this ambivalence that the strange composite was created in the first place. Or take the word *"Schöpfungswelt"* (creation-world), a not particularly uncommon word in German. A non-German analyzing this word would probably say that *Schöpfung* (creation) and *Welt* (world) are two nearly identical concepts, and suspect here only an empty pleonasm. But for a German it is not a pleonasm; for him it signifies a world full of the richness of creation, a creation in constant cosmic evolution; it means the eternal and continuous operation of creating, the breath of God the Creator in the world. This multivalent meaning is deliberate, and German syntax makes it possible, since the composite word is not just an abbreviated summary, as it is in English; rather, both parts can be understood as reciprocal attributes. Joyce had to invent new words to give them multiple meanings; but in German, the syntax provides for this, and the composite word just represents its extreme case: in truth, a fluctuating, floating meaning runs through all German words once they are placed into a sentence. A translator who does not take account of this kind of fluctuating "formal" content in its syntactical construction will not do justice to the spirit of the German language and will produce poor translations.

I should like to include here an incidental remark, because to me it seems so completely persuasive; it has to do with the almost baffling phenomenon of German music. How is it possible that a people who have one of the most unmusical languages of the world have been able repeatedly to produce musical geniuses of such cosmic creativity? How is it possible that within the supposedly unitary German spirit, the musical and the unmusical exist in such close proximity? Certainly the German spirit is not deficient in inconsistency, but inconsistency often enough points to a common consistency that can be discovered behind it, and the German opposition of unmusical language with the most sublime music points this out: Both these modes of expression are primarily content based on form, they are both based almost exclusively on their syntax, and both lend their "vocabulary" that fluctuating, indeed dynamic meaning that is never simply at rest, but radiates, so to speak, openly and on all sides. By virtue of their form-based content, music and the German language are examples of the same symbol type. German philosophy was born out of the same spirit, and Neo-Kantianism, as represented most recently by Cassirer, is eminently suited to this spirit, so it is no wonder that it has produced a theory that assigns symbols their meaning and importance rigorously in terms of relative position within a system, that is, as perceived by the Logos.

We may ask what this has to do with the translator; the answer is, quite a bit. Up to this point we have been speaking just of translation *per se*, not mentioning that we have meant all along the translation of literary works. If we had merely been concerned with translating business letters, documents, and the like, documents written in simple discursive language, we should not have needed to go to all this effort: We would only have needed good dictionaries and grammar books to get a reasonable, adequate result. But "reasonable" and "adequate" are not acceptable in a work of art. Every artwork is an organic, systematized whole — this is its most essential trait — and thus its use of words reflects the whole of the language that gave it life, the language in which it is cast. As an example of this we quote a very simple poem, the "Abendlied" (Evening Song) of Matthias Claudius:

> Der Mond ist aufgegangen,
> Die gold'nen Sternlein prangen
> Am Himmel hell und klar;
> Der Wald steht schwarz und schweiget,
> Und aus den Wiesen steiget
> Der weiße Nebel wunderbar.

Let us assume someone wanted to translate this verse into English:

1. Looking up *aufgehen* (from *aufgegangen*) in the dictionary, we find "rise," "evaporate," "open," ("as a door, but also as a blossom"), "come loose," "untwist," "untied," "consumed," "mathematically contained without a remainder," etc. All these meanings overlap in German in this single expression; the factual differences that English attaches so much importance to, and which it highlights with its large and diverse vocabulary, are disregarded in favor of a deeper commonality. On looking a little closer, one can see this commonality; it is that of a semi-abstract, soundless event, in which something (here too the German is multivalent) is set loose, dissolved, even redeemed. Almost the main thing here is that silence, but what is meant here is not an earthly silence, but a silence that is metaphysical, unearthly. To be sure, the phrase *"Der Mond ist aufgegangen"* is a completely ordinary expression, in itself banal, which can be easily translated as "the moon has risen." But since a real poem, as we have here, reflects the entire organism of a language, it cannot confine itself to this one meaning: It has to give a sense of all the other shared meanings suspended in the word *aufgehen*. Not only has

the moonlight appeared in the heavens (risen),[6] but it has opened up there like a blossom; indeed it is almost like an infinite door to the depths of the night sky (open), and in its waning (evaporated) beams, it not only loosens (untwists) the hard facticity of the world, but brings it and all the problems of the world into a state of total and perfect release, even redemption. And all this takes place in an inviolable silence. German deliberately includes all these meanings; using its syntactic construction for this very reason, it has formed the many meanings of the word *aufgehen,* and it is the job of the poem to make this intent clear, one might say, as clear as moonlight. The declarative function of German is overtaken by its poetic function; only in the organic completeness of a poem, where the sentence has become a single poetic word, so to speak, can that sentence be grasped in all its fullness.

2. The second line contains a poetic trick, loosely connected to the syntactic character of German. If this line had read *"Die gold'nen Sterne prangen"* (the golden stars glitter), it would just be kitsch. That gold glitters is of course a worn-out phrase, which would have applied as well to "golden stars," if these had not been transformed with a stroke of genius into the diminutive *Sternlein,* or little stars. English does not really use the diminutive, and even the French diminutive ending "ette" and the Italian "li" are not completely comparable to the German "lein" and "chen": The German diminutive does not simply express smallness, but also — and here we have the fluctuating, floating quality again — a non-rigidity, a childlikeness, a non-frightening quality. In short, "lein" in particular expresses the feeling of a fairy tale, thus, something quite specifically German. Claudius has chosen "lein" here, and by combining the childlike, fairy-tale feeling of *Sternlein* with the rigid Baroque formulation of *goldprangen,* he hints at the loosening, redemptory quality of the whole image.

3. In the third line, on the other hand, German syntax is at work

---

[6.] Broch writes the parenthetical English words into the original: "risen," etc.

again; with *"Die Sternlein prangen hell und klar"* (The little stars gleam brightly and clearly) all is as it should be: *Hell* and *klar* serve as adverbs. But that is not what the poem says; it has inserted the words *am Himmel* (in the heavens) between *prangen* and *hell und klar,* thus giving *hell und klar* also an attributive, appositive function beyond their adverbial meaning. Thus, the meaning also evokes the image of a "brightly clear night sky" *(Himmel hell und klar),* that is, precisely that sky which, on the one hand, is the locus of the "risen moon," and, on the other hand, is completely consumed by *(aufgehen in)* moonlight, as well as opened up *(geht auf)* by it. Not till now is the first line completed, and only here does it reveal its multiple meanings. This effect comes from three peculiarities of German word-formation and usage that are dictated by syntax and thus closely related to each other: Firstly, as opposed to other Indo-European languages, German tends to place the object as close to the subject as possible, to frame it between subject and finite verb, as if to demonstrate, in anthropomorphic terms, how the object, both as thing and as word, gets its form from the system. Secondly, since the verb is postponed to the end of the sentence, the adverbial modifier usually following it is likewise postponed. This rule is so rigorously observed that the verbs themselves, when they are fused with their adverbial prefixes, are inverted and dismembered, so that just the adverb *(auf)* here, e.g., in "Der Mond geht abends am Himmel auf," actually winds up at the end of the sentence. Thirdly, adjectives used adverbially (with a few exceptions) have unmodified forms identical to adverbs, not least because they are given identical syntactic treatment, namely, placed at the end of the sentence. All this is highly confusing to a non-German, to whom this sentence structure with its verbs torn apart seems barbarous, and identical forms for adverb and adjective seem just plain incorrect. If one wanted to construct the second and third lines of our poem along English lines, it would be something like: *"Am Himmel droben prangen golden die Sternenhauf"* (In the heavens above gleam golden crowds of stars), but for all its unambiguous correctness, it would not be a poem in any language.

The first three lines depict heavenly events, the next three, their earthly counterpart:

4. We need not comment further on the adverbial construction *steht schwarz* (stands blackly); we would just be repeating ourselves. But this does not keep us from delighting in the *"und"* that follows it, to which the second predicate *"schweiget"* (is silent) is appended, leaving no doubt as to the adverbial use of the word *schwarz,* an essential part of the first half of the predicate. Nor does this exhaust the function of *schweiget.* In those highest heavenly spheres in which the stars are gleaming and the moonlight is beaming, above the layer of clouds and thunder, there abides such absolute stillness that it need not specifically be mentioned; and it is just as silently inherent in the word *aufgegangen* (risen). But if the earthly silence here is to reflect that in heaven, it has to be mentioned specifically: So the forest neither rustles, murmurs, nor whispers, but rather, it makes the sound of silence using the active verb *schweiget* (to say nothing), to express this stillness. In this tranquility it gazes up at the heavens, "standing darkly" *(schwarz stehend),* including and reflecting this stillness in itself.

5. This reflective idea dominates the fifth line as well. From the *Wiesen* (meadows) that are the real counterpart of the heavenly fields, a white mist *(der weiße Nebel)* rises *(steiget);* this earthly stillness, nearly as soundless as that in heaven — but white, not transparent or "clear" as above, as a sign of its earthliness. This mutual reflection is much more strongly expressed in the word *"steigen"* (rise); the moon rises as *geht auf,* but the mist rises as *steigt auf.* In *aufgehen,* as we have said, there is something abstract and removed, whereas *aufsteigen* is related to earthly, concrete things like *Stiege* (staircase) and *Steg* (footpath). Instead of this heavenly release, this dissolution of boundaries, instead of total fulfillment and revelation (as with *aufgehen*), *steigen* retains only the single meaning "rise," an unambiguous, concrete upward motion, appropriate to the moon, when thought of as a concrete object on the horizon; but the word *aufsteigen* contains none of the metaphysical grandeur imbuing the whole event.

6. It is no accident that the "white mist" stands in the last line. For here, at the end of the verse, something special takes place; one might almost say that here is where poetry really enters in. The key word is *"steigen,"* which correctly needs its adverbial completion with *"auf"* (i.e., *"aufsteigen"*), so that with the appropriate inversion and dissection of the verb, the line would read *Der weiße Nebel steiget auf.* If we wanted (just for fun) to "correct" the little poem, our "emendation" would look something like this:

> Der Mond ist aufgegangen,
> Am Himmel droben prangen
> Golden die Sternenhauf';
> Der Wald steht still und schweiget
> Und aus den Wiesen steiget
> Der weiße Nebel auf.

In this non-poem, *aufgehen* and *aufsteigen* would be in parallel, but Claudius, being the poet he is, does without pedantic parallelism. Instead he sets up quite a different kind of parallelism: He replaces the appended prefix "auf" with the adjective *wunderbar* used as an adverb, which fits with *hell und klar* in the third line not just because of the rhyme but because the rhyme strengthens the parallel structure. Because of this parallel syntax, the same process unfolds in heaven and on earth: There, the stars shine *hell und klar* (brightly and clearly), and heaven itself is *hell und klar* (bright and clear); here the mist rises *wunderbar,* wonderfully, and the mist itself is *wunderbar,* wonderful; on both levels the adjective/adverb modifiers have been brought into beautiful (yes, wonderful) harmony. We are first aware of the "wonder" of the world beyond when we see it reflected in earthly life; only when things are freed from earthly causality do they become "wondrous" [*Wunder*], and before this wonder can be manifest, the metaphysical question must "arise" [*steigt hinauf*], so that its solution can be revealed [*geht auf,* or open up] from above. The German *wunderbar* contains the two

English ideas of "miracle" and "wondering," and even if both meanings are retained in "wonderful," which means both "astonishing" and "exceptional," it is nonetheless translated much better with the German *wundervoll* than *wunderbar*. With *wundervoll*, as in English, the meaning remains factual and earthly, while *wunderbar* reveals the apotheosis of mere earthly beauty into unearthly splendor. And this is just what the Claudius poem does: By replacing the final "auf" of *aufsteigen* with *wunderbar* at the poem's end, it reaches back through all six lines, back to that parallel moonrise at the beginning, and gives the moon its *wunderbares Wandeln*, its wondrous walk through the heavens — it paints the whole with the wonder of heavenly moonlight.

We said at the start that there are no unnatural symbols. We also said that symbol-languages are organisms that generate vocabulary units with organic, internal affinities but that also have syntactic relationships, by virtue of which they incorporate these vocabularies into the whole and make them usable as speech. Further, we said that the relationship of those vocabulary units, as form based on content, derives from the organism as a whole selecting or rejecting them, while their syntactic coherence, no less formative as a system, takes these same words and gives them content based on form. It is only natural that the same thing occurs with an artwork, a poem, or with any organism that has developed in an equally natural fashion. And in fact the six lines of Claudius show clearly how the poem's selection process works, and what kinds of connections it sets up between the words it has selected. Moreover (and this is probably truer of German than of any other language), it is evident from all this how the poem has a manifestly systemic coherence, a syntactic unity controlling the whole poem. This coherence is so strong that all the so-called poetic licenses, such as replacing adverb-prefixes with adjectives, can be traced to this deeper stringency. All this the translator must keep in mind when he ventures on his task.

But even this is not enough. In these six lines we have met the fairy-tale side of German-language morphology, and it seems to be worth noting that this was within a song: for songs are part fairy tale, and fairy tales are part song. While fairy tales and songs exist in other cultures, too, their specifically German versions are closely interconnected. Recalling what we said about the German diminutive, we may perhaps conclude that the intimate forms of fairy tale and song transform whatever is dangerous and frightening in the Logos into something harmless, innocuous, even *gemütlich.* For behind fairy tale is myth, and behind the song is music *per se:* Both reflect the greatness and the danger inherent in the Logos. The Logos contains curse and blessing alike, and while on the one hand, its freest and purest areas of development, that is, philosophy and music, lead to the highest achievements of the human spirit, in everyday life, on the other hand, its apparent logic often leads to false conclusions, promotes nonsense to sense, and robs humanity of its wisdom, so that falling back into chaos, it turns fearful and treacherous. The Indo-Europeans, not just the Germans, are the people of logic, and all their myths, not just those of the Germans (though they are unfairly blamed for this), reflect the inhumanity of man in chaos, trying to avoid the snares of false logic by cunning and deceit, treachery and violence. But while other Indo-European nations found their way back to wisdom through contact with other cultures, particularly the Mediterranean ones, the German spirit did not. Along with its great philosophic achievements it has fatal weaknesses; along with the profundity and breadth of meaning of the German language there are the hazardous attractions of its vagueness, ambivalence, and specious precision. And no matter how well this German spirit knows the dangers menacing it, no matter how profoundly, powerfully, and fearfully it is conscious of the chaos that lurks within itself, still it takes as much pride in this chaotic profundity as in the Logos, of which it thinks itself, for this very reason, to be the sole legitimate representative. And thus it considers itself entitled to its tiresome arrogance, the arrogance with which it dares to bother (to put it mildly) people of a different type, who have learned to temper their logic with wisdom. Yet this aggressiveness is also a product of fear, and if they do not act out this fear externally (and there have repeatedly been such periods in German history), they must calm it from within. This is when the German tells himself that the dangers he senses within himself are not so bad, that the fateful power of myth cannot drive him to violence and self-destruction; this is when he tells his fairy tales, when he sings his songs. And so a grace arises out of his curse, the grace of the diminutive, which hints at the great in the small, the powerful in the most intimate, the mythic in the fairy tale, the harmony of the cosmos in a song — the German poem. The forest is dark, ready for night; but off in his faraway lair, the dragon still dwells, at peace now, too, but a dragon nonetheless. In the white mists the elf is weaving, a wraith in the moonlight, yearning for rest, but an elf nonetheless. There is something of all this in every work of German poetry, and the translator must take it into account if he is to understand the spirit of the German language.

Hugo von Hofmannsthal and His Time: Art and Its Non-Style at the End of the Nineteenth Century *(1947-48)*[1]

translated by Michael P. Steinberg

THE essential character of a period can generally be deciphered from its architectural facade, and in the case of the second half of the nineteenth century, the period of Hofmannsthal's birth, that facade is certainly one of the most wretched in world history. This was the period of eclecticism, of false Baroque, false Renaissance, false Gothic. Wherever in that era Western man determined the style of life, that style tended toward bourgeois constriction and bourgeois pomp,[2] to a solidity that signified suffocation just as much as security. If ever poverty was masked by wealth, it was here.

[1] Hermann Broch, *Hugo von Hofmannsthal and His Time: The European Imagination, 1860-1920*, translated, edited and with an introduction by Michael P. Steinberg (Chicago: University of Chicago Press, 1984), pp. 33-81. Footnotes are by Steinberg.
[2] The terms *Bürger, bürgerlich, Bürgertum* present a common but always exasperating translation problem. They cannot be consistently translated as bourgeois and bourgeoisie. The German word *Bürger* differs in tone and evaluation from the French

1. RATIONALITY AND DECORATION

Rationalism[3] often goes hand in hand with an enjoyment of life, for anyone who thinks rationally is likely to believe, in addition, that what is
enjoyable in life exists to be enjoyed. On the other hand, rationalism
demands a sober, clear, unadorned, and realistic view of the world, and
assures the quick discovery that the cruelty and horror of life stand in
the way of an untroubled enjoyment of life. In order to attain a full
enjoyment of life, either one must transfigure what is horrible into
beauty — like the Romans with their gladiator games, like a Nero or a
Borgia — or one must keep one's eyes shut in the face of ugliness and
cruelty, and distinguish the beautiful so that it becomes an aesthetic
"elect" and makes possible undisturbed pleasure. Yet whether it is one
or the other, whether the affirmation of cruelty or its negation, despite
the rationalistic demand for the unadorned, it is a question of an aesthetic overadornment of the ugly, of its hypertrophy or oversweetening.
It is a question of denial concealed by "decoration."

The nineteenth-century bourgeois was just as rationalistic as the
Roman; like the Roman he built world empires and war machines. But
he was neither a Nero nor a Borgia. For that he considered himself too
humane, and to a certain degree he even was. When he cosmeticized
and transfigured his world so that it became capable of affording him

---

bourgeois; the former connotes "solid citizen," the second, "philistine." In general,
where Broch describes a German or Austrian context and merely intends to define the
class, I have used the words burgher and *Bürgertum,* terms common to books on central European history. Where his context is pan-European or where his tone is pejorative (and these two most often go together), I have used the word "bourgeois." As far
as the adjective is concerned, Broch most often uses the term *bürgerlich* in a pejorative
manner, and I was thus able to translate it as "bourgeois." In natural German usage, the
adjective *bürgerlich* is more pejorative than the nouns *Bürger* and *Bürgertum.*

[3.] By "rationalism" Broch refers not to the rationalist tradition in philosophy but to a
kind of instrumentalism, and essentially a false system of thought. It is a Nietzschean
usage. Thus in "Culture 1909" he had written, "Rationalism is the mode of thought of
experience . . . it is a disguise of the spirit, not the spirit itself."

enjoyment, he did so by concealing all its misery. His passion for decoration was more hypocritical than that of his crueler predecessors, and this brought him the hatred and scorn of Nietzsche, a hatred that would have certainly grown even stronger, had he witnessed the bourgeois's turn to cruelty. No, at that point the bourgeois was not yet cruel, even if he was already preparing himself to become so: for in all aestheticism, in all decoration, even the most harmless, there slumbers cynicism — itself just as much a product of rationalistic thinking — and there slumbers skepticism, which knows or at least suspects that it is merely a sort of "transfiguration game" which is being played.

Where decoration is not naive but the result of rationalism, it is not free creation but artificial, sometimes of good quality, but artificial nonetheless. And, moreover, since it is skeptical, it has no footing of its own, but needs models. Rationalism is earthly, and is on the lookout for earthly prescriptions. The Romans found their earthly norms in Greek art, the Renaissance in antiquity as a whole; and in the Enlightenment the process repeated itself. The rationalistic outlook — directed at extant reality — nearly always leers backward in order to uncover in some former earthly reality the rules it needs for an evaluation of the present; it becomes eclectic.

For, as a consequence of his rationalism, nineteenth-century man was individualistic, romantic, and accordingly also historicizing. The discovery of the individual came about for Christian Europe in the late Renaissance, indeed through the very set of mind *[Geisteshaltung]* that also led to Protestantism: the supraindividual, the Platonic, above all the ecclesiastical as spiritual community was suddenly perceived as something upheld by earthly, visible man, and hence not only something which had to be kept alive by him but something in need of his constant renewal. The individual, with his earthly, individual soul, was placed heretically at the center of the universe in order that he, the measure of all things, might also be the measure of all divine validity. Outside the church, however, this is the attitude of romanticism, the source of its greatness as well as its demise, and the source of its historicism. Since it is here that the earthly-private, the personal, even the intimate are to be raised to a universal significance, and in the end this universal reveals itself once again as the everyday, the romantic view must ratify itself by virtue of the sublimity of those human accomplishments which extend from the past into the present. The superhumanness required by romanticism is projected into the historical so that it may in its turn be retrieved for the present.

In any case, it becomes clear that polarities so dear to historical interpretation, polarities such as rational/irrational, collective/individual, classical/romantic, present-minded/historicizing, etc., represent mere shifts in the center of gravity, which, though they correspond to logically indispensable dialectical motions in the development of the value systems by which human life is determined, have very different periods of variation, so that they can appear in multifarious combinations. The Middle Ages, for example, were theologically at least as rational as modern science — even magic has rational foundations, all the more so a mysticism in the mold of Eckhart — and were nevertheless far removed from any kind of individualism, historicism, or decorativism. Conversely, despite its highly rational basis, romanticism veers with ease into the irrational, as soon as the historicizing elements it contains gain the upper hand. Thus, any attempt at rigid schematicism is wrong. Otherwise in the final analysis one is bound to find that classicism, in view of the romantic schemes of rationality, must be itself irrational. History is saturated with countless polar-dialectical undulations, and the styles of particular periods are nothing other than manifestations of interference produced by the coincidence of such undulations. And it is no different in the case of the conditions of the style or non-style of the nineteenth century, in which rationalism, individualism, historicism, romanticism, eclecticism, skepticism are all embedded and sustained in a kind of Manchesterism calculated for all eternity, all converging in an inextricable bond, yet each retaining an organic unity. Realism is not a style but, rather, the fulfillment of the claims of rationality. And inasmuch as every age thinks rationally in its own fashion, that is to say considers itself rational, all genuine art is realistic in the end; it represents, in its own specific vocabulary, the picture of reality of its time.

Clearly the non-style of the nineteenth century is also a style — there is not one product, not one piece of furniture of this most style-forsaken epoch that does not reveal at first glance the decade to which it belongs; and, accordingly, this non-style too expresses a specific epoch-reality. The vocabulary it employed, in literature as much as in the visual arts, was a stringently realistic one, namely the vocabulary of a naturalism, bound to earthly surfaces, which renounced everything decorative, wanted nothing to do with hypertrophy, oversweetening, or any kind of romantic sentimentalizing, and, wishing to express things as they appeared to it without adornment, grasped them at the point where they made the impression of being least adorned — in the depiction of society.

The naturalism of earlier centuries was principally associated with painting, a medium inadequate for the new social naturalism, inasmuch as painting could serve it with mere social caricatures, in other words with something that is neither wholly pictorial nor wholly naturalistic. The graphic or pictorial social caricature — like the short story — is tied to individual situations, which permit it at best to intimate the social totality but never to represent it in its entirety. To do the latter requires a broadening of the scope of exemplification, and this is achieved when the social totality is mirrored in the totality of a human life elapsing within it; just as, conversely, a life can only be grasped in its entirety when the corresponding social totality is depicted. This is precisely what is accomplished by the novel and, in the main, only by the novel. The epic (whether that of antiquity or of Dante) was concerned with the totality of the universe, Greek tragedy with the totality of fate's dominion. And if, thanks to Shakespeare, drama won a multidimensionality that encompasses every human aspect (and not least the totality of an individual life), even here, indeed even in *Hamlet* (and not unknown to Shakespeare), the stage opposes itself to everything that proceeds beyond its own most characteristic level of action: only the immediate conflict in which the hero finds himself is significant; his past and even his future (though the entire dramatic tension may be directed to it) do not — in the truest sense of the word — play a part. Epics, like dramas, are essentially anti- or at best a-individualistic. Only with the novel — the Italian novella was still to a great extent preindividualistic — only with Cervantes does the totality (one could almost say lyric totality) of the individual attain a comprehensive portrayal, inwardly and outwardly unfettered, suited to psychology and society. The novel was prepared, as it were, to be the art form adequate to the nineteenth century and, by means of its individualistic naturalism, to flower to its full maturity.

It was, for all its opulence, a thoroughly gloomy flower, one that sprang from urban ground. The world city, which after the collapse of the Roman empire had seemed gone forever, was suddenly resurrected; London and Paris, joined a little later by Berlin and New York, had become world metropolises; and it was natural not only that the expression of the time should evolve inside them, but also that all their qualities should adhere to it: their multifariousness, their scatteredness, their greed, their gloom. No matter how the novel in its ostensible unadornment confronted the city — whether it let itself grow to the gigantic realm of Balzac; whether it fulfilled itself in the sinister world of Dickens; whether, in Zola's hands, it formed itself into dreams of hope for all future romanticism; whether, the opposite of such an expanse, it unraveled itself, through Flaubert's intense eye, into a ghostly backdrop to the stirring of a single soul; or whether, having degenerated into a mere erotic novel of society and its idiocy, it could and still can turn even the unadorned into adornment — the novel remains relentlessly overshadowed by the gloom of the city.

But why was this sort of gloom never transformed into its opposite? Why did it persist, and why did it never find relief in a truly satirical novel? Why did the urban gloom of the nineteenth century preclude the sort of work so masterfully achieved by Voltaire and Choderlos de Laclos, Laurence Sterne, Jonathan Swift, to say nothing of the monumental satire of Cervantes and Rabelais? It is more than anything else satire itself and satiric structure, which can be held responsible. For satire in its innermost being is after all polemical and (in a broad sense) political, and the great age of politics, the age of the formation and consolidation of the European states, in short that most eminently political age of the Baroque, had been stilled forever with the Congress of Vienna. And if Baroque politics were still practiced as a form of art — a form of high art, which like all art had something frivolous about it — and could indulge in the laughter of satire, the age that followed and the social problems it contained were, quite simply, deadly serious. One has merely to compare drawings by Hogarth with drawings by Daumier; one might claim — *cum grano salis* — that the former are dramatic and political, the latter epic and social; the former are for the most part grounded in the burlesque of the individual situation, the latter are always aimed at the social totality and are consequently thoroughly gloomy. Where then, as in the novel, the social totality in its full reality achieves (or merely purports to achieve) expression, satire can scarcely have a part. The novel was certainly capable, though rather infrequently, of achieving humor, but in general it remained overwhelmed by the gravity of the epoch — and this as a direct consequence of its realism.

Nevertheless, lively satire still existed in the nineteenth century, if only as the heritage of the eighteenth century; it survived in the theater.

IT CONFORMS, politico-socially and dramatically, to both dialectical conceptual polarities that the theater stands in a structurally natural consanguinity with the Baroque, whereas the nineteenth century by virtue of a similar relationship brought the novel — which it discovered for itself—to its maturity.[4] All the same, polarities invariably prove themselves unreliable, and the result in this case is the opposite of what would have most naturally followed from them: not the novel, but rather the theater, and beyond that the opera, at least as far as its external aspects are concerned, became the representative art form of the epoch. With the theater, the eighteenth century reached into the nineteenth, just as the principle of Baroque theater construction remained exemplary, now as before.

Theater is makeup. It could never have made use of the naturalistic unadornment to which the novel aspired (but which not even the novel could attain). Indeed, the daring breakthrough engendered by Stanislavsky's genius at the turn of the century promoted totally new scenic possibilities, but they were not those of the total naturalism he intended. In the nineteenth century, notwithstanding the insignificant dilettantism of the Meininger Hoftheater,[5] there was no breakthrough of that sort; the theater could never have risked it. After all, the theater, as long as it wants to remain a whole, must address the entire public; to a far greater extent than the novel, it has a social and economic function. The

---

4. "Es entspricht den beiden dialektischen Begriffspolaritäten politisch-sozial und dramatisch, dass das Theater in einem strukturhaft natürlichen Verwandtschaftsverhältnis zum Barock steht, während das 19. Jahrhundert, kraft ähnlicher Verwandtschaft, die Romanform, die es für sich entdeckt hatte, zur Blüte gebracht hat." The way this sentence reads in the German, and the way I have translated it literally into English, the "conceptual polarities" are not identified. They are not the polarities of theater-Baroque and novel-nineteenth century, first because these are identified as the phenomena to which the polarities correspond, and second because each pair is in itself not a polarity. It is very possible that Broch intended the phrase "politically-socially and dramatically" to contain the referents of the "conceptual polarities"; perhaps they should be read as adjectives rather than as adverbs, in other words as "political-social and dramatic-[epic] conceptual polarities." These categories make perfect sense in the context of the discussion of the previous paragraph.

5. Meininger Hoftheater: celebrated German theater under the direction of Duke Georg II of Saxe-Meiningen which toured Europe between 1874 and 1890. See Max Grube, *The Story of the Meininger* (Coral Gables, Fla.: University of Miami Press, 1963).

"people" *[das "Volk"]* of the nineteenth century most assuredly read no novels — least of all, since they were looking for "something beautiful" in art, novels depicting mass society and misery. And even if this type of novel ever gained the acceptance of the bourgeois and his bad social conscience, especially if it reached him in a tasteful, romantically scintillating guise, he always considered the reading of novels a carefree summer pastime, best left to his female appendage. In short, for all its social airs the novel was banished to the sidelines. The theater, on the other hand, ensnared everyone, the bourgeois along with the "people," the former especially with the incentive of preferential orchestra stalls, while others had to make do with the gallery. And for that very reason the bourgeois, seated beneath the ecstatic gaze of the "people," found in the theater all the decorative beauty that he — not only he, nay, the entire epoch — required, in order to satisfy the demand for a secure, in part ceremonial, in part carefree enjoyment of art and life. Of course, these are superficial symptoms, but symptoms nonetheless, and behind them looms the "stylistic indifference" of naturalism, its incapacity to create its own style, an incapacity which like all others reveals itself in the unerring testing ground of the reality of the theater.

Amid the eclectic conglomeration of styles which made up the non-style of the nineteenth century, the theater, or more precisely, the art of the actor, was the sole domain in which a true stylistic tradition continued to flourish, and because it was a tradition, it was not eclectic. It was Baroque art; during the classical period it had acquired a certain simplicity and breadth, and it was this that was practiced with an almost noble rigor at the Comédie Française and the Vienna Burgtheater.

This high dramatic art was in conflict with its repertory, in almost natural conflict. Its tradition was rooted principally in France, schooled on Racine and Corneille, and if its power of expression was hardly sufficient to master ancient tragedy, it was certainly strong enough to amalgamate quite perfectly Shakespeare on the one hand and, on the other, the works of the great German writers of the Weimar period. To all that, the tradition was adequate, and it found no successors in the late nine-teenth century. Grillparzer[6] was a last straggler, whereas Hebbel[7] belonged to an entirely new type of production, one that indeed still considered itself classically conservative and tradition-bound, as it treated principally historical and, hence, political themes, but one that in truth had long since fallen away from that tradition — how could it have been otherwise? — and now occupied itself exclusively with specif-ically bourgeois concerns. In France this change had been swifter. For although French drama, much to the benefit of its effectiveness on the stage, held on so conservatively to its own peculiar technique, which it only now developed into supreme virtuosity, it was nevertheless so broadly influenced by naturalism (that is, also by the city and its gloom), that it was able to cast off its historical costuming and become the Sardouesque society-piece, which, regardless of its generally aristo-cratic cast of characters, revealed itself as a pure product of the bour-geois spirit and the bourgeois problematic. Whether its action was based on erotic or — however exceptionally — other motives, this drama no longer mirrored the ethical (and thus in the broadest sense political) superiority of the hero in victory and defeat, but rather his social success and failure, all the more so as psychological interpretation came increas-ingly to supplant moral foundation. Thus the sphere of duties of the actor which the classical repertory had staked out was extended into entirely unfamiliar territory, one which had nevertheless to be exhaus-tively traversed; if the theater wished to remain alive, it had to confront such unfamiliar tasks.

The confrontation came about by way of an intensification *[Über-steigerung]*. Of all the realism and naturalism once offered to the theater

6. Franz Grillparzer (1791–1872): the most celebrated Austrian classical poet and dramatist, whose 1840 play *Dream as Life (Der Traum ein Leben)* was, along with Calderón's *Life Is a Dream* (La Vida es Sueño), the inspiration for Hofmannsthal's *The Tower.*

7. Friedrich Hebbel (1813–63): northern German playwright who settled in Vienna.

in the hues of romanticization, there remained nothing; for, elevated into the superrealistic and supernaturalistic style of an old-fashioned heroic scene, the theater achieved a new and hence more genuine reality. A style of theater, modeled — now as before — after kings, usurped the domain of the bourgeois, transformed the bourgeois problematic into that of a royal drama, transformed bourgeois existence into royal existence, turned bourgeois successes and failures back into victories and defeats, and was able to do so, was compelled to do so, because this method of acting had moral intentions and therefore had to make visible a moral, human background, even where it had to reproduce bourgeois issues and their psychologizing structures. And this was essentially more than the fulfillment of another one of those fantasies forever fostered by the bourgeois who would see himself as a king. To be sure, it was "transfiguration-drama," but insofar as it was genuine drama, the transfiguration — into the human — was also genuine; it was genuineness achieved by means of intensifying the nongenuine and the decorative into the essential, a genuineness that lay, so to speak, on the frontier — one step farther, and the conversion of the decoratively nongenuine would undergo yet another dialectical transformation, namely, into the operatic. No wonder an epoch filled with the insatiable desire for decoration sought and found its highest representation precisely in the opera.

On the stage, the non-style of the period became a style again. In the truest sense, or the most correct double-sense of the word, the theater became the showground of the epoch's poverty, masked by wealth.

2. THE TURN AWAY FROM DECORATION

Nevertheless, the breadth of late nineteenth-century culture and civilization, the multiplicity and substantiality of its corresponding artistic expression, is far from exhausted by the formula "poverty masked by wealth."

What in fact took place outside — or really in opposition to — this style of the period, and yet was in every manner and form connected with it, born from it and raised with it, and nonetheless aspired at the same time to dissolve it (any organism is ambivalently faced with such processes) — this was surely no less important, indeed if anything more important, than what was happening within its own more narrow framework. For in, and in spite of, Second-Empire Paris, far from the splendid caryatides of the Haussmann facades, far from all official art, far even from the most accomplished art of the theaters, but no less far from the practiced forms of naturalism and especially from its romanticism, indeed often in conscious opposition to this last, there arose — quite miraculously — a new art: on one hand, the new French poetry inaugurated by Baudelaire, averse to all superficial naturalism and, more especially, to every kind of romanticizing, and, on the other, impressionism, an autonomous outgrowth from the foundations of painterly tradition, void of any literary influence, certainly the legitimate heir to naturalism, yet bearing within it from the start a revolutionary, antinaturalistic kernel.

Every genuine work of art is at once new and bound to tradition: later generations see before anything else its place in tradition and thus grow increasingly blind to revolution, whereas contemporaries (for their part blind to tradition) see in it only the unfamiliar and the new: for the general public an insolence meriting punishment, for the artist a revolutionary act, all the more so since he considers that its success depends on newly discovered insights and resources of artistic technique. The mastery of geometric perspective and its applicability on canvas: this was Dürer's pride, and the impressionistic pride is presumably to be found in the optical, physical knowledge of the fundamentals of color-producing, color-produced shades of light. Yet artistic revolutions — and certainly one as brilliant as impressionism — are autonomous; they themselves can make use of scientific discoveries provided they are themselves suited to revolutionary purposes, but they cannot be caused by them. Artistic revolutions take place when preexisting conventions of symbolic language are thrown overboard, and art sets to work once more to search for primal symbols, with which to build a new direct language aimed at attaining a higher artistic truthfulness; this alone is at stake in art.

Not at one stroke, but step by step, it became clear to the impressionist painters that the impression of reality which a painted picture can transmit depends on two medial layers: the first is the medium of light, which makes objects visible and awakens them into being, forms their shapes with its shadows, colors them with its refractions, envelopes and outlines them one and all with its impenetrable transparency. The second is the medium of the flecks of color applied to the canvas, which (themselves dependent on the light) are by virtue of their arrangement, distributions, nuances, and contrasts, capable of forming symbols, symbols which can indeed only be referred to the other medial layer, that of light, and are never intended to be more than symbolizations of light, but, because of this very integrity, penetrate the light-induced reality of objects. In other words, painting has always to be reduced to the media of light and flecks of color, because any visual commentary about the reality of the world must take place exclusively between and upon these two medial layers, and, by such a reduction of the painting process to its ultimate nakedness, its most naked, primal principles will provide access to that sphere, from which the primal symbols of art and hence new truths arise. This and nothing else was the revolutionary discovery of impressionism, and in this and no other way can impressionism be defined: it was a new attitude toward object reality; it discovered the medium as reality.

Yet is this mode of perception confined to painting? Does not the representation of reality always and everywhere require a medium? Painting is the expression of reality, a specific language in which visual reality is brought forth, but does not the same hold true for every language, for the language of speech as much as those of music and painting? And behind all these communicative potentials of the reality symbol, does there not stand an ideal, Platonic language as the last, and precisely Platonic, vessel for reality? The most recent phenomenological and positivist linguistic investigations lie entirely in this direction; indeed very often expressly analyze the "phenomenon of the medium" as such. And when they become metaphysical, as above all in existentialism, and want to break through the impenetrable medial layer, for the purpose of grasping an "immediate reality," they consistently find behind it — nothingness. Art, on the other hand, is allowed, nay, more than that, is enjoined, to practice metaphysics: without a concern for reality, there is no genuine art! For only the producer of reality, namely art, and only art, can and may raise this concern with the aid of its primal symbols, which in turn become accessible to it only — as impressionism exemplifies — when the metaphysical concern is addressed. Indeed, metaphysical necessity is graduated in accordance with the different artistic media. The language of painting occupies a sort of middle ground between those of music and speech, for in music one apparently finds a convergence of the level of symbol and the level of musical reality — of "meaning" and "meant" — whereas the process that leads to the symbols of words and precisely to the poetic must undoubtedly pass through a whole sequence of other medial layers, and can thus only be understood as a symbol of a symbol of a symbol, etc.; hence the wish to extract primal symbols from the medium of the word appears all but hopeless. And yet even this is not completely hopeless: it is no accident that it was through a contemporary of the impressionist movement, Baudelaire, that language attained individual life and meaning, extending far beyond the mere function of communication to the point where language, in gratitude, as it were, for its newly received devotion, becomes itself a source for the conception of reality, the poetic conception of reality.

Baudelaire's relation to language is certainly not lacking in mystical infusions, since mysticism indeed proclaims itself everywhere in his work; yet fundamentally it is not a mystical relationship but a technical one. By the same token, the impressionist painter is no mystic but a technician of the phenomena of light and color. Yet fanaticism for truth always has something mystical about it; hence an artist who directs all his strength toward an artistic truth, to the "correct" solution of his problem of light and language, presumably has the right to call himself a mystic, a mystic of his own artistic technique, all the more since this very attitude has produced a most specific phenomenon: *l'art pour l'art.*

L'art pour l'art has always existed. Every honest artist, and for that matter every honest craftsman, has been and remains under an obligation to it, and there is nothing mystical about it. On the contrary, it is a thoroughly rational attitude, and during the nineteenth century — not unlike its logical and social counterpart "business is business" — it acquired if possible an even higher rationality, all the more so after the shift in artistic orientation away from the central value of religion and the church. And what was an art which, like impressionism, defined its notions of truth exclusively from its own peculiar medial layers, to do with an orientation toward goals that lie outside such a framework? All this combined to make the notion of *l'art pour l'art* typical of the nineteenth century and, moreover, to imprint on it an entirely typical trait, namely, that of "social indifference": neither does this art seek to address social themes, nor does it seek to insinuate itself into the social fabric as a gratifying, instructive, uplifting, or otherwise marketable product. Clearly this does not mean that "success" has become irrelevant to the *artiste pour l'art;* but his relation to the "public" has altered nonetheless. As long as society remained grouped around a central value, art had, so to speak, a natural place within it; artist and public were unified from the first as to the kinds of themes and modes of representation that would prove either admissible or inadmissible. Yet with *l'art pour l'art* that harmonious relationship was transformed into one of antagonism and violation. The artist tries to convert and to violate the bourgeois, and knows in the process that it is an almost hopeless undertaking, that the bourgeois will calmly let him starve, and that one must hence consider oneself lucky, if — like Cézanne — one is able to put aside all momentary ambition and direct everything to future success. For posthumous fame to exceed fame is a phenomenon previously unknown in the history of art.

It is in this manner that *l'art pour l'art* thinks itself and wishes itself to be posited outside every society and, above all, outside every bourgeois society, and yet forgets, in doing so, that no one, not even the artist, can leap over his own shadow: the artist's very opposition to society places him within its framework, precisely as a heretic can only exercise a meaningful function within the church; outside it, that function becomes simply meaningless. *L'art pour l'art* and "business is business" are two branches of the same tree. Whether one has feelings of harmony or of discord toward the society in which one lives, as circumstance and problematic one cannot escape that society, and it is that society which implants the same social indifference in the unsuspecting bourgeois and in the artist alike. But when the bourgeois clings to his business principles with a rationally grounded and unassailable unconditionality, and is blind to anything that might possibly repudiate them, and when the artist with the same unconditionality clings to his own artistic principles, both act in the same way both logically and sociologically, and in both cases the unconditionality of social indifference intensifies to a state of genuine cruelty; in both cases it is the cruelty of bourgeois society, a cruelty which it is true was bound to be surpassed as dictatorial society stripped the last shackles from bourgeois humanity.

And this very cruelty explains the antagonism that reigns between the bourgeois and the artist. Not that the bourgeois was overly affronted by the crass and cruel naturalism of art. No; he may remonstrate with it a little, since misery appears to him as unsuited to enjoyment, especially when not sufficiently romanticized, but in the end he accepts it nonetheless, for it produces no guilt feelings in him, he does not know that he is exploiting misery, and there is no realm of misery for which he feels himself responsible. Not even the representation of the social totality, as in the novels of Zola, can rouse him, to say nothing of the partial representations of which painting is capable. Moreover, impressionism retreated far from social description. Paintings like Manet's *Balcony* or *Theater Loges*[8] have nothing to do anymore with the social efforts of a Millet, a Courbet, etc., and the idyllic lyricism of most impressionist landscapes must surely have been thoroughly pleasurable to the romantic bourgeois sensibility. Why then the furor at the Salon of 1865 over Manet's perfectly lovely *Olympia?* Why this unsuitedness for enjoyment? The answer is relatively simple: the social descriptions of naturalism had shown the bourgeois what he was doing and the base deeds he had committed, whereas the *art pour l'art* of impressionism showed him what he was and yet did not want to be. For not in its themes but in its mode of representation, this art — even if it may once again appeal to later generations — proclaims that the unconditional cruelty of the epoch is making itself ready and yet is already present.

The bourgeois practices his cruelty, whether consciously or — more frequently — unconsciously, directly on his fellow man, especially when the latter is of more feeble economic capacity; the artist's cruelty, on the other hand, although no less unconscious, is sublimated in his work. The more the impressionist *art pour l'art* developed, the more clearly this tendency to cruelty was brought to light; the paintings of Cézanne, Gauguin, and van Gogh, the poems of Baudelaire, are in their acute directness (and certainly not in their harmless themes) nothing but cruelty, unconditionality, inconsiderateness, harshness — all in the purest sublimation. This has not the slightest thing to do with the private tendencies to cruelty of a Baudelaire or a Gauguin, just as, in the converse process, van Gogh's private (and alas so futile) efforts for a socially helpful life did not relieve the cruelty of his paintings one iota. Even the

---

[8.] Broch seems to be referring to a painting called *A Loge at the Théâtre des Italiens* by Eva Gonzalès, a pupil of Manet's. It was completed in 1871, exhibited at the Paris Salon of 1874, and currently hangs in the Louvre. I am grateful to Ilene Shaw for this reference.

wish that haunts every artist, the wish to *épater le bourgeois,* although it plays a part, is clearly of no consequence, not merely because social logic dictates that the *épater le bourgeois* will find himself on the same plane with the *bourgeois épaté,* but, much more, because the bourgeois will accept every *épatement* as long as it seems harmless to him, i.e., as long as it remains rational. Within the bounds of the rational he will permit any hypertrophy of the "ugly"; it thus becomes a "Grand Guignol" for him, in short, something he can perceive as legitimate romanticism. Yet the *Fleurs du mal* are unacceptable to him. For the cruelty brought to consciousness within the poetry (with complete poetic unconsciousness) reveals the utmost horror: the irrational in itself.

L'art pour l'art guided art back into a totally irrational sphere, and that was its great accomplishment. Like everything great it contains the moment of necessity, a rationally derivable necessity at that: just because the rational principles of this naturalism-turned-impressionistic attained their utmost radicality in the absolutism of *l'art pour l'art,* it was doing this frontier, which one may well call a frontier of infinitude, that the dialectical reversal into the opposite, into the irrational, was bound to occur. For every approach to an absolute contains qualities of infinitude, and all infinitude contains qualities of the irrational. This is the point at which mysterious depths open up: the abyss of the human soul, of human existence, the abyss of the world. And for that very reason every reversal into the irrational threatens to become a reversal into the anarchical as well; anarchy lurks constantly in the depths. It is not only the bourgeois whose security has been threatened who shrinks back in terror here; the artist himself hesitates, and how could it be otherwise? Will his power of sublimation still be equal to the new mission assigned him? Will he not have to conjure an additional sublimation in order to conquer the radically unknown, the anarchical, a sublimation of which neither he, nor indeed art itself, will be in any way capable? To be sure, even great masters like Monet, Renoir, Degas, to say nothing of a Pissarro or a Signac, no longer risked this leap into the unknown but remained in the sphere of the known — i.e., in a mode that was already on the way to establishing itself within the known and even to being able to command a public. Manet had taken the first step; the second, the breakthrough into the totally irrational, was reserved for Cézanne and van Gogh, and only very seldom in the history of art — probably not since Michelangelo and Rembrandt — has the irrational presented itself with such vehemence as in the works of these two artists. With Cézanne and van Gogh, impressionism overcame its naturalist heritage.

Where the irrational shows itself with its full vehemence, it does so in the form of primal associations and primal symbols. The world is seen once again for the first time, and with an immediacy otherwise known only to the child and the primitive (and accordingly to the dreamer, if with different coloration); hence the expression of the world becomes that of the child, the primitive, the dreamer; it fulfills itself in the creation of a new language. The achievement of Cézanne and van Gogh was to create a language, and even if it had its origins in the impressionist vocabulary — indeed it would have been inconceivable without its groundbreaking medial symbolism — what sprang up was nevertheless something totally new: the primal symbolism of an irrational, immediate vision of the world. This was the very same upsurge, the same sudden presence, as the one which, three decades earlier, had made audible Baudelaire's primal sound, his primal vocabulary, the same recklessly cruel unconditionality of the primal as Baudelaire's, the same primal stare of primary existence. If Baudelaire and his successors — including Verlaine, Rimbaud, Tristan Corbière, Péguy, even Mallarmé (though just barely) — still reveal certain impressionist, naturalistic, and romantic touches, it was the primal association reawakened by Baudelaire that was once more placed face to face with language. And the power of primal association — which is precisely what precedes all linguistic creation — continued to function: in the shadow of his work, poetry after Baudelaire created a new language within the French language, a language which, mainly under Mallarmé's guidance, developed to an ever more acute constructiveness, and thus — like all painting after Cézanne — became, in an astonishing manner, more and more suited to represent the essence of being, the essence of man — i.e., to transform the irrational into a new, acutely precise rationality.

This was the artistic revolution at the close of the nineteenth century, and, seen from the outside, it was a quite harmless, quite restricted revolution of a few artists in the out-of-the-way province of *l'art pour l'art*. Nevertheless, this breakthrough of the irrational did not stand alone in the sweep of time — there are no isolated phenomena. The superrational nineteenth century had everywhere begun to "irrationalize," not last in its intoxication with machinery and production. The fact is that at that time a pleasant state of suspension still governed, one in which nothing had yet been decided, and where the possibility still remained that the threat of anarchy festering within the irrational could be tamed. The taming did not succeed, could not succeed. For new symbols, new languages are generated by a new breed of men, and such a breed had announced itself in that new art of the nineteenth century. The revolution of spiritual expression, ostensibly restricted to art alone and hence ostensibly harmless, was an initial symptom of a world-shaking whose end we cannot perceive even today, and the artists of that time, themselves full of artistic self-discipline, were heralds of anarchical dissoluteness, forebears of the new breed of men. The twentieth century was to become that of the darkest anarchy, the darkest atavism, the darkest cruelty.

THERE is no doubt that *l'art pour l'art* conclusively discarded the decorative mission previously assigned to art. With its tendency toward the undecorative, indeed the antidecorative, *l'art pour l'art* has no desire to fulfill any sort of social function; it wishes to be asocial, is often even antisocial, yet cannot refrain from forcing its products on the public. What kind of social role, then, does it seek to assume?

Where primal associations, primal vocabulary, primal symbols are at stake, where the irrational enters a work, mythos does not seem to be far away, and in fact deep in the unconscious of every art — every great art — there slumbers the desire to be allowed to return to mythos and once again to portray the totality of the universe.[9] It was in mythos that all human history began, in mythos — i.e., in the poetic language of its epics — that those primal associations, that primal vocabulary, that primal symbolism first took form, and each new historical epoch has since rediscovered them for itself, even if in varying forms; in other words, it was in mythos that every new epoch created for itself an adequate language, together with the new creative symbols suited to it. Should not an epoch of the most powerful breakthrough into the irrational — like the present one — be capable of advancing back into mythos? Clearly, poetry and painting, in whose territory the impressionist breakthrough into the irrational fulfilled itself, had never previously been the true domain of mythos, but does that mean it must forever remain that way? Moreover, this kind of breakthrough into the irrational must necessarily expand, must little by little seize every branch of artistic expression, and not remain restricted to a single one — was not the novel, then, as the specific artistic genre of the nineteenth century simply predetermined to be seized by it? In this role, the novel may once again provide the irrational with a partner of the sort it had not had since its encounter with epic in primitive times: is the breath of great epic not already evident in the works of a Balzac, a Dickens, and does not the choice of subject, a century later, in Joyce's *Ulysses* and Mann's *Joseph* indicate the approaching fulfillment of a development which from the beginning had aspired to mythos?

With Zola, the minstrel of rationalism, of the age of the machine, of

9. I have translated the term *Mythos* as "mythos" rather than "myth" for two reasons. First, Mythos/mythos refers to the quality of myths rather than to the actual stories; second, the English "mythos" retains the positive and poetic connotations of the German word as opposed to the potentially pejorative connotations of "myth." Mythos, especially for Broch, refers to a state of truth rather than to a fabrication.

socialist man, the idea of the modern mythos had already assumed a distinct form — without of course being realized. His naturalism remained undisturbed by the breakthrough into the irrational of contemporary *art pour l'art*. Yet even the case of Flaubert is hardly different, even though his perfectionism of form was at least common to impressionistic and postimpressionistic poetry, from Baudelaire to Mallarmé. It is with Joyce that the picture first changes, for his ambition is focused purely on the mythical. Notwithstanding the mythologizing structure which to a large extent Joyce gave to his novel of a day and a night, and notwithstanding the symbolic wealth which, by dint of his polyhistoric genius, he was able to compile from the total range of human ontogeny and phylogeny and incorporate into his work so as to increase its mythological weight, it was Joyce who truly realized — and this is by far the most essential point — the conjunction with impressionism. Joyce eavesdrops on language and languages, in order that they out of gratitude might supply him with the correct world-symbol and with this the essentials of reality, and such linguistic mysticism (by contrast with which Flaubert's becomes schoolmasterly pedantry) is nothing but a resumption of the medial method invented by the impressionists — and is every bit as rational. For all true mysticism is rational, and linguistic mysticism is mysticism of the medium. And, just as with the impressionists, the breakthrough into the irrational emerges here; it is to be seen and felt everywhere in Joyce's work, sometimes, as in the chapter "Anna Livia Plurabelle," roused to the greatest intensity. Yet the analogy with impressionism goes even further: as little as impressionism, whether in painting or in poetry, actually became mythos, so little was Joyce's success; even here the naturalistic system of coordinates remains undisturbed, and in the end the story remains a representation (often even a romantic one) of Messrs. Bloom and Finnegan, though certainly in an accomplished comprehension of their living totality.

Even such highly developed novelistic art proves itself unable to attain the rank of mythology. Why is this so? Is it simply because of its

naturalism, without which living and social totalities cannot be compre-
hended? No, the causes must lie deeper, and they do. It is not only that
every late-developing art which sets about to recapture the irrational
must — in order to do so — undertake a break with tradition, which is
exceedingly difficult (the impressionist revolution is a prime example of
the intricacy of this sort of process of detachment), and it is not only that
there can be only partial detachments, simply because nothing can ever
totally escape from its own epoch and the effects of its traditions — all
this stands in strict opposition to the mythological function as such.
Mythos breaks with no tradition, because no tradition precedes it, and
it adheres to no tradition, because logically and temporally all tradition
begins within it; whatever paths of development tradition might have
established, however diverse may have been the branches that grew out
of it or continue to grow from it, no matter whether they tend toward the
irrational or rational, artistic or scientific attitudes and modes of knowledge — all these paths together are fundamentally indistinguishable as
one single unity embedded in the mythical germ-cell. This is an unre-
peatable situation, and can least of all be restored atavistically, so to
speak, with the help of a breakthrough into the irrational. And this holds
true more than ever for such a late form of expression as the novel.

In short, with inadequate means, namely those of naturalism, the
novel pursues an unattainable end, namely the mythical. And yet means
and end are simply insolubly linked. The novel, incidentally, assumes
the same relation to myth as postimpressionist painting does to primitive art. Both naturalistically impeded in their artistic wills, that is, by a
naturalism which belongs to all styles and is hence forever incapable of
providing them with a style-building symbolism indispensable to all
great art, they were both ultimately forced to orient themselves to a primitive art, which adhered to no style but in its mythical unity is the source
of the formation of all style. Joyce and mythos, Gauguin and primitive
art: one like the other revolves around the realism of early art, its "primal
naturalism," with which it endeavors faithfully to delineate the world

and human existence as it sees them, and in the process reaches beyond the naturalistic into the essential. For primitive man, unencumbered by any expressive tradition, is capable of grasping what is "essential" to him, capable of expressing it with total purity, unburdened by any outside influences, and it is precisely here that the style-producing strength of his "primal naturalism" lies. Every genuine style signifies the accentuation of a world-essentiality, signifies the transformation of chaos into a system of essential elements; yet only the "primal style" of the immediate beginning also possesses the naiveté of an absolutely undiluted realism, that naiveté which is at the same time the most highly and — as with Homer — the most refined artistic intellect.[10] It is artistic intellect and nonetheless suitability to nature, it is the style of nature itself, which reveals itself in the art of the immediate beginning, and the more advanced the evolution, the more seldom do reminiscences of this glorious, truly mystical naiveté emerge. They emerge surely not with Gauguin, yet they do with Henri Rousseau, surely not with Joyce, yet probably with Kafka.

Figures like Kafka and Henri Rousseau are unique not only on account of their genius but more because theirs was a genius that succeeded — in the center, so to speak, of European artistic tradition and hence of contemporary art — in keeping itself almost entirely free of tradition. What is remarkable and enduring about them would have been less striking outside their environment, outside the European mainstream. Certainly, at the time of Henri Rousseau and Kafka there was no longer a no man's land beyond the bounds of tradition, yet in the nineteenth century such a periphery unquestionably existed, for Russia and America were still peripheral countries. All the influence of central and western Europe notwithstanding, these were "youthful" countries,

---

[10.] Artistic intellect: *Kunstverstand.* In translating *Verstand* as "intellect" I have followed the example of Hannah Arendt's translation of this Kantian term. For a discussion of that very translation choice, see Mary McCarthy's Editor's Postface to Arendt's *Life of the Mind* (New York: Harcourt Brace Jovanovich, 1978), 2:24–45.

countries of the "beginning," not of course a mystical beginning but one in which tradition could be and indeed was newly endowed. Where American poetry became autochthonous, as with Herman Melville and later with Whitman, there surfaced, even if merely by suggestion, that primal naturalism from which primal associations, primal vocabulary, primal symbols had once arisen. Thus the naturalism of Tolstoy stands closer to that of Melville than to that of Zola, however much it may surpass the social breadth of the American. For monumentality — and this is here the *tertium comparationis* — entails not so much social breadth as social depth, and the latter is a function of the choice of symbol. The characteristic of monumental art is not a wealth of symbols, it is rather the single essential symbol, the symbol which in a single image, in a single twist of fate, grasps and subsumes a totality along with all its limbs; the rape of Helen is an event whose symbolic power stamps the total fate of the Greeks and Trojans into a single, common inalterability, and Melville's vision of the hunt for the white whale, the vision of lonely seas and lonely worlds, the vision of infinite inalterability, reveals more than a single seafarer's fate, and the war portrayed by Tolstoy is the one which from time immemorial has been relentlessly foisted on mankind in terrible helplessness. Where narrative is guided by a symbol of inalterability, structures develop which in their innermost composition can be accurately measured against the greatest epics of world literature, indeed, against the greatest myths.

Nevertheless, no mythos evolved. Be it Tolstoy, Dostoevsky, or Chekhov (who demonstrated, contrary to Western narrative art, that a genuinely satirical epic is possible): all of them drew the ultimate conclusions from the realism of the novel and, indeed, forged ahead to its frontier of infinitude, i.e., to the frontier of "primal naturalism," the boundary at which the naturalistic prepares to turn into the essential; nevertheless, the novel remained the novel. And even if these masterworks have long surmounted the nature of the bourgeoisie from whose non-style and narrowness they emerged, and even if their concern is no longer the bourgeois, although he is portrayed, no longer his problems, although they are dealt with, but, simply — especially with Dostoevsky — a grandiose metaphysics unfolds whose irrationality has only little in common with the Joycean breakthrough into the irrational, for all that, the distance from the mythical is no smaller than with Joyce. In short, even here the bounds of the novel cannot be overstepped; here also the "inadequacy of the means and the inaccessibility of the end" are brought to light. And even here, precisely here, the novel remains in that curious hybrid state in which it is a work of art that is never able to rise to the rank of perfect art, the rank of style-creating "perfect poetry" which is the property of lyric poetry, drama, and not last, precisely of the great epics. Contrary to these, the novel is not a producer but a consumer of style, not a subject but an object of style, and the symbolism it creates falls into utter triviality, becomes an accessory. In other words, the task which was assigned to the novel directs itself principally, now as always, to its duty to represent the totality of life, and with far less intensity toward its duty as an artistic creation. Balzac is more important for the novel than Stendhal, Zola more important than Flaubert, the formless Thomas Wolfe more important than the artist Thornton Wilder: the novel does not stand, as does true poetry, under the measure of art but under the measure of "writerliness," and even the monumentality of the Russian epic is now as before implanted within the region — so utterly characteristic of the nineteenth century — of apoetical and at times almost antipoetical *belles lettres*.

Does this mean that the new artistic tradition of the nineteenth-century Russian epic was not sufficiently radical? Or does it mean, rather, that the criminal, bloodthirsty Nazi intellectuality was right when it maintained that only after a gloriously atavistic self-annihilation of the world would a new mythos first be able to rise from it — the Nazi mythos of the twentieth century?

A concern of this sort will once again suggest the attempt to anchor mythos in the irrational, in this case even as an apology for atavistic murder. Once again, then: mythos cannot be identified with the irrational, yet neither can it be identified with the rational; it is rather both these combined, and is consequently greater and more pregnant with meaning than the mere sum of its united parts. Man's development, however, consists of the progressing autonomy of individual rational attitudes, and thus removes itself further and further from the mythical unity of once upon a time. Even the poetry of Dante, born in a far less divided epoch than the present one, can no longer be described as mythical. Yet the Italian Renaissance of 1300 was surely no less radical than that of nineteenth-century Russia.

It is not on the mythological maturity of the world that this depends — that is the Nazi aesthetic — but on the turning away from the decorative mission of artistic endeavor and on the emphasis upon its ethical duty. Here, however, one further commonality is revealed between the poetry of Dante, which prevailed over the decorative *Minnesang,* and the great Russian epic; both rediscovered the ethical within the inalterable, just as the Attic tragedy of fate had done, driven by the necessity of humanizing the intensely terrifying fatalism of the Homeric mythos. The cognitive goal of poetry, its goal of truth, is no longer simply the beautiful in its compassionlessness, no longer solely the reality of fate; above and beyond that, it is the reality of the soul and of the struggle against fate which it must wage if it wishes to remain human. In this manner the novel, and precisely the Russian novel (as opposed to the Western, e.g., Joycean novel) broke through the boundaries of *l'art pour l'art,* and up into the open: it flung open the door to "the ethical work of art," it at last became political, indeed it even achieved satirical possibilities (Chekhov), and, although "merely" a novel, although mere *belles lettres,* although — as a result of its naturalism — not really style-creating, it rose to a valid aesthetic representation of the epoch, which the West had achieved only in the theater — and that indeed only as an ersatz, because Western narrative art, despite its adequacy to the times, was not able to raise itself above the romantic, above the psychological, above the decorative nature of its bourgeois origin.

3. THE VALUE VACUUM OF GERMAN ART

From the West and from the East came the factors that determined European literary and pictorial expression; Germany, which between 1750 and 1850 had earned a decisive right of codetermination, had practically nothing more to contribute.

Interpreted mythistorically (which is clearly not admissible), it is almost as if the German spirit had known that with Goethe and Hölderlin it had exhausted itself for a long time to come, and that artistically, or more precisely poetically — curiously enough, painting had been long lost — it was condemned to silence. Grillparzer, surely a playwright of extraordinary stature, a historical intellect of the first rank and a totally worthy heir to Schiller and Kleist, did remain prominent into the new era, but his place soon became vacant, all the more so when Hebbel, far too much an epigone to fill the breach, claimed his inheritance. It was different, however, with poetry, where it was still practiced as true literature — in remote areas, in the provinces, in crotchety little bourgeois towns. Here one must single out Gottfried Keller and Conrad Ferdinand Meyer, and also, though at a certain distance from them, Theodor Storm and the Austrian Ferdinand von Saar.[11]

The European significance of recent German literature was now totally lost. There was a sole exception: Nietzsche. The lonely summit he claimed for himself and which has since been reduced to platitude was truly his own; there he stood, he alone, separated from all the lesser spirits. Yet he did not want to be included in the ranks of literature, least

[11.] Ferdinand von Saar (1833–1906): Austrian social realist who ridiculed Hans Makart in the 1904 novella *Der Hellene*. See Carl E. Schorske, *Fin-de-siècle Vienna: Politics and Culture* (New York: Alfred A. Knopf, 1980), pp. 299ff.

of all German literature. And for this very reason he was as German as one can be German. Because, despite his powerful artistic temperament, he remained aloof from art and poetry, and — apart from a few poems which, significant as they are, remained completely secret — felt himself to be an exclusively rational thinker, he merged perfectly into the new posture of the German spirit. The mystical causes that had rendered poetry forbidden ground to the Germans had their effect on Nietzsche too.

The causes may have been mystical; for the reasons there are explanations. The fact that the people stripped the poet and thinker of his poetic domain, and that this happened exclusively to the domains not of the thinker but of the scholar and the musician, can be traced at least in part to the radicalism of which the German spirit is often — unfortunately all too often — capable. By virtue of this radicalism, the German spirit developed one of the principal features of the time, its rationality, to the extreme, to extreme abstractness. And in such abstractness, only the sciences and music remain as justifiable means of expression. In fact, the revolutionizing quality of the epoch was in the first place scientific — even the impressionist revolution in painting points in this direction — and there is hardly a field of science to which Germany in the second half of the nineteenth century did not make the most significant contributions; in the field of music not only had the strongest impulses once come from Germany, but now too the most significant revolution was introduced by Wagner.

But why then did Germany's so-called "take-off" period *[Gründerzeit]*, the years 1870–90, create the impression of a total intellectual void?

In literature and painting, in fact, nothing at all was produced, and scientific revolutions, which for the most part take place in the seclusion of laboratories, libraries, and studies, are seldom so turbulent as to be observed by more than the narrowest circle of colleagues. Who, for example, was aware at the time of the revolution in scientific axiomatics being prepared in the work of Gottlob Frege and Georg Cantor — not to mention the fact that work of this kind penetrates a wider circle of knowledge. The situation is clearly different in music; here there was no stagnation as there was in literature and in painting but, rather, a genuine revolution, one that proceeded not in isolation and hiding but in all openness, turbulently, noisily, and arrogantly, and aroused just as turbulent and noisy an opposition, so that it could actually have brought about the disappearance of the "value vacuum," as the condition of these decades may rightly be called. Why did the vacuum nonetheless have to persist? Why was it only after the epoch had passed that Wagner — and for that matter his immortal antagonist Nietzsche — were granted standing and lasting currency? The allusion to Cézanne, who allegedly sold only one painting in his lifetime, is no answer; a much more reliable answer lies in the radicalism of the German spirit, expressed also in its revolutions (and which in the political sphere makes monstrosities of them). Above all, the explanation is to be found in the revolutionary work of art itself, that is, in the very mechanism of revolution.

REVOLUTIONS are tuned to the "new." And both science and art, as forms of knowledge, would be nonexistent were they not unerringly aimed at the new. But revolutions demand the renewal of the "whole," and for this reason there are relatively few scientific revolutions in the true sense; scientific novelty is most often the product of "progress," i.e., the patient, logical, step-by-step probing into the riddle of the world totality, which must be wrung ounce by ounce from "supplemental" knowledge. Art, however — and its individuality and its justification lie in this opposition — is impatient: it contains neither something "supplemental," nor any true "progress"; rather, it must strive with each and even the slightest work — if it is to become a genuine work of art — for an immediate grasp of the world totality. For this reason its development proceeds exclusively in revolutionary thrusts.

Yet when a work of art truly grasps the world totality, it embraces along with it *eo ipso* the period of its own formation. Science is hardly capable of anything similar. A Cézanne still life, for example, at least for anyone who is not totally dense, makes one breathe the entire atmosphere of the turn of the century (and it does not even have to be a Cézanne); whereas the theory of relativity, which in 1905 — as one of the few scientific exceptions — was a revolutionary event, requires truly complicated theoretical-interpretive feats of analysis if it is to be taken as a statement about the entire structure of the spirit of the time. Science does not burden itself with understanding the period of its formation, yet the moment it crosses the boundary between theory and praxis, it has a direct bearing on life, in that by dint of its own needs it awakens new needs and so becomes a crucial factor in the growth of a new epoch, in the creation of the "historically new." The artist, however, the genuine artist, does not concern himself with the needs of the epoch, yet he feels and knows what it is and wherein its novelty lies, knows this thanks to an intuitive insight that one might simply call the "feel for the epoch." Though he lives in the midst of a confusing multiplicity of a myriad anonymous and petty events which fill out and constitute the epoch, he is able nonetheless to grasp it as a whole; he grasps it, so to speak, from "the inside out," and as it is the new epoch which thus enters his work as a totality, the epoch becomes the "new" in his art. The average man (and with him the average scholar — also, indeed, the artistically motivated nonartist) is seldom faced with the same situation; he remains submerged in the anonymity of the events which surround him, and for him the epoch first loses this anonymity when it has expired, when he can view it from "outside" as a historical unity and whole. When a new period has established itself, the preceding ones reveal themselves as historical wholes.

This, however, is also the mechanism of so-called artistic "success." A work of art that reproduces the entire content of an epoch (and not only its style) and consequently presents something uncannily "new" to its contemporaries, will most often achieve a status of familiarity only after the period has passed; that is, it will be first understood and acknowledged when the period of its origin has become a historical whole. This occurs most often with the emergence of the succeeding generation, which actually shapes the beginnings of posterity, so important to the artist. In other words, the major work of art usually only achieves a lively currency at the "edge" of its epoch, whereas the minor work, that is, the one that neither grasps nor wishes to grasp the totality of the epoch but satisfies itself by serving the epoch's needs, i.e., in being a part of the structure of the epoch and its style, is usually extinguished at the close of the epoch. The phenomena of obsolete art and belatedly acknowledged art are reciprocal.

In the middle of an epoch, two main groups of artwork share between them public acclaim: first the products of transient, "minor" art (which is often simply non-art), and second the kind of major art that stems from the previous or an earlier period and has already succeeded in crossing the threshold of understanding. These curious bedfellows are the backbone of the opposition to a period's contemporary major art, an opposition that grows necessarily sharper the sharper the revolutionary claim of the new art.

When a political, social, or economic vacuum has set in, its corresponding political, social, or economic revolution is not far away, and the more complete the vacuum, the more the various "partial" revolutions — as they simultaneously sharpen their tendencies — will converge in their struggle to become a single, all-encompassing revolution. The same holds true for artistic revolutions, and the major work of art that carries them is what clearly reveals the total mechanism, through its position and especially through the counterrevolutionary opposition it evokes. For if an epoch totality is centered in a value vacuum, the major work of art in which it finds its expression must also express that vacuum. The work of art becomes the mirror of the vacuum, and in doing so vindicates its revolutionism, yet at the same time immediately arouses counterrevolutionary opposition — must arouse it, because a mirror that shows the vacuum is an uncanny thing, and even the man who manages to live in the vacuum cannot endure the sight of it. This is what occurred in the second half of the nineteenth century, with particular acuteness and radicality in Germany: the Wagnerian artwork was big, remains big, and is the mirror of the vacuum.

JUST as the style of the time — above all where it was determined by romantic naturalism — was a non-style, so was Wagner an unmusical music genius and, moreover, an unpoetical poetic genius. He was precisely the genius of the vacuum, and where the genius is interrupted — because no genius can be constantly a genius — it reveals a non-style in the worst possible abomination, in the form of empty bombast, as in the Faust Overture, or of empty sentimentality, as in the Wesendonck Songs. But Wagner also possessed the naiveté — in part carefree, in part refined — of a genius. He knew that works of art could be made from any material, provided an architectonic appropriate to the material was employed, and, theater genius that he was, he knew that the theater and opera of his time already contained the elements that could be used — intensified into the superromantic, superrational, and even, when necessary, into the untheatrical and the antitheatrical (e.g. *Tristan*) — in the construction of the necessary vacuum architecture. It was a question of constructing the so-called *Gesamtkunstwerk*.

This was the proving ground for Wagner's special feeling — indeed his positively unerring instinct — for the epoch. He knew that the age he was born into would choose the operatic as the form for its representative total expression; he saw how the new bourgeois cities were seeking a community center that would replace the cathedral and how they strove to raise the Place de l'Opéra to that honored status — and all this red-plush, gilded, and gaslit ceremoniousness corresponded to his own blueprint for the tasks of modern art. But he knew also that opera in its present form had not met the demands of such ceremoniousness; for that a Meyerbeer was not sufficient, however esteemed he may have been by the public and by Wagner himself; for that, not even a Verdi was sufficient, to say nothing of the otherwise routine repertoire, which consisted exclusively of superannuated romanticism and would have been altogether intolerable without the insertion of ballets. Aware of all this, Wagner knew very well that his plan for an operatic *Gesamtkunstwerk* would satisfy a genuine need of the time. On the other hand, it was far less clear to him that a plan that is supposed to serve the immediate needs of its epoch, and thereby reap immediate success, will possess all the characteristics of "minor" art and will be condemned from the start to remain in the style of its time, which here means in its non-style, in the false truthfulness that imprinted its indelible stamp on the Wagnerian life and work. Whatever happened, it was rational and romantic, naturalistic and ceremonial, sentimental and gloomy, catholicizing and mythologizing, and above all (despite *Die Meistersinger,* and perhaps there more than ever) perfectly humorless, as humorless as only a vacuum can be. Nevertheless it was major art, had become major art, and was able to unite all the disparate elements of the non-style into a single style, the specifically Wagnerian style — one could almost say brew them together, because behind the scenes stood the radicality of genius which, with utter, radical shamelessness, exposed the nakedness of the vacuum.

Wagner was rejected and assailed by his contemporaries, and the reason, as usual, was blindness to a major work of art; as usual, the assailers thought that it was non-art (in this case non-music) that they were dismissing. Of course Nietzsche, who launched the most significant, indeed the only significant attack, saw deeper, for he was Nietzsche, and he saw through Wagner because he saw through the epoch, saw through it with hatred and scorn because he saw into its vacuum. And whereas in his own work, which he looked on throughout as an ethical and ultimately metapolitical work of art and hence a conclusive representation of the epoch, he raised the epoch to utmost clarity so that some day by virtue of such clarity the vacuum might be overcome, he saw justifiably in the emergent Wagnerian work, with its similar claims of representation, the exact opposite of his own. None of the contemptible and odious inclinations of the epoch are combated in it; none of its hollowness, its specifically German hollowness, is brought into the open; no, nothing of that was allowed to be touched, for it was needed as the basis for theater, as the requisite of a theatricality with which the inarticulately hollow, mystical, patriotic, and decoration-craving appetite of the philistine German public could be tickled and gratified. For Nietzsche, then, Wagner offered no synopsis or comprehension of the epoch but was, rather, one of its attending components, a minor artist who had strayed into the gigantic, a mere opera composer who dared to break with the main operatic tradition because he felt himself incapable of furthering it, and against whom the minor Bizet had to be posited as a major counterexample. Yet did this not shift the discussion to another track? Was Nietzsche not unintentionally attending to the affairs of the anti-Wagnerian music philistines? He was indeed, just as half a century later — surely against his will even in death — he was forced to serve as a spiritual pretext for the affairs of the philistine beast.

In other words, when discussion is limited to the sphere of music, we no longer have the seer-philosopher Nietzsche confronting the fundamentally unprophetic Wagner, but a fundamentally nonmusical genius confronting a music genius, even though an unmusical one. And Wagner is thus attacked where the musically philistine public were wont to attack him, and where he, vis-à-vis this public, was just bound to be in the right. The public (and one dares not say perhaps even Nietzsche as well) had preferred Liszt to Wagner, but Liszt knew how far his genius son-in-law had surpassed him. The public — and this with a mite more justice — had preferred Verdi to the antimusician Wagner, but under Wagnerian influence Verdi found the style of his old age and created *Falstaff,* his most splendid work. The public treated Bruckner and, a little later, Hugo Wolf, the two most genuine and profound musical geniuses of the epoch, just as badly as it had treated Wagner. In

symphonic as well as song literature, it preferred the strictly conservative, tradition-bound Brahms (probably to his detriment), but he was
more and more eclipsed by the work of Bruckner and Wolf, and their
styles are both unthinkable without Wagner.[12] Even if we were to dismiss the revolutionary in Wagner as too rational, it was precisely
through this rationality that he acted as the necessary catalyst for the
musical revolution that he initiated. For Nietzsche, despite all his clair-
voyance, this was absolutely inconceivable.

Yet why, we may ask, did a genius like Bruckner, who was well able to
stand on his own two feet, need a catalyst for his development? The
somewhat childish personal reverence he extended to the master of
Bayreuth is surely not a sufficient explanation; for all the reverence, a
Bruckner needed no kind of support from Wagner or from anyone else.
He did, however, need the world, the world totality, the epoch totality, to
whose expression he as an artist was called and bound and which,
despite his search for it, he was probably unable to grasp once and for
all, although, artist that he was, he had surmised not only it but its
vacuum as well. Locked into his solid Catholic beliefs, in which there is
no value vacuum, Bruckner was first made aware of the world, the
epoch, the vacuum through the Wagnerian work of art; in the art of the
vacuum he found the worldly stance that could serve as the point of
departure, from which for the first time he could gather the world up to
the higher state of his own work, overcoming the vacuum and surpassing Wagner. Of course, it could be objected that Bruckner was unique,
but did not something similar occur in the case of Hugo Wolf? If his was
a unique case, it was a paradigmatic one, paradigmatic for the unique-

[12.] Broch's evaluation of Brahms follows the traditional late nineteenth-century
dichotomy of Wagner the revolutionary versus Brahms the conservative. This view
was first challenged in Arnold Schönberg's groundbreaking essay "Brahms the
Progressive" (*Style and Idea*, 1950). For an account of the battle about Brahms, see
Peter Gay's essay "Aimez-vous Brahms?" reprinted in *Freud, Jews, and Other
Germans* (New York: Oxford University Press, 1978).

ness of a world caught in a value vacuum, paradigmatic for the uniqueness of Richard Wagner, in whom this vacuum was uniquely embodied.

The value vacuum of the world presented an extraordinary situation. In Germany it had adopted forms more visible than anywhere else, since intellectual production was reduced almost completely to the fields of science and music, yet that does not imply it was not visible elsewhere. The cruelty, for example, that emerged with increasing intensity in impressionist and postimpressionist painting can be taken as a symptom of vacuum. For even if every value vacuum is primarily a break in the flow of tradition, an empty spot in that "patchwork process" by which epoch styles are generated, each in the womb of the preceding style — though they develop in mutual dependence and influence through the revolutionary rejection of this "mother style"— this is still, so to speak, only the technical view, the "historico-mechanical" view of the problem; in truth, a particularly ethical phenomenon stands behind it. In the nineteenth century, the dwindling of the old European systems of beliefs had begun, and with the collapse of this central value, the splintering of the comprehensive religious value system gave rise to autonomous individual systems (of which *l'art pour l'art* was one). In other words, the universality of the governing ethical attitudes began to disintegrate, and the desires they had until now ethically subdued began to be unleashed. Here, however, the circle closes: every value vacuum is an incitement to revolution, but for the fulfillment of revolutions the unleashing of desires is indispensable.

Nietzsche was aware of the mechanism of the value vacuum and of this superimposition of epochs (the union of which appears to be a historical law), and he was aware of the sinister consequences slumbering within them, all the more so as he could see Germany, burdened with evil, before his own eyes. Wagner knew nothing of this; for him, every potential vacuum was always filled by the *Gesamtkunstwerk;* and the *Twilight of the Gods*, in reality a glorification of German being and German fate, was a theatrical apotheosis whose carryover into life could be at most an unfulfillable wish. But those who followed, the philistine beasts, were no longer able to differentiate between the ethical *no* of the prophet and the *yes* of the theater aesthete, so that Nietzsche and Wagner, in a strange communion, bore the spiritual responsibility — presumably distasteful to the former and pleasing to the latter — for the shameful events which after not too long a time were to rock Germany and the whole of world civilization.

4. Vienna's Gay Apocalypse of 1880

In Vienna, too, the value vacuum ruled from 1870 to 1890, but whereas in Germany these years constituted the "take-off" period, here they constituted the "roast chicken era" *[Backhendlzeit]* and were therefore taken as lightly as befits a vacuum.

Were there such a thing as a complete value vacuum, man would be reduced to the level of the melancholiac, for whom life is not worthwhile. But there is no complete value vacuum, and although the stagnation of artistic value production is no isolated phenomenon but portends a non-style encompassing all areas of life, that non-style will not commonly be considered by its contemporaries as a detriment to life. There remain sufficient realms of activity into which life values can be projected, and substitute values are usually by far the most gratifying. Daily life always continues. Germany in the "take-off" period had a full and overflowing daily life and not only created within it genuine scientific values but was also so busy with the construction of its ominous economic and national dimensions, that it could easily disregard both value vacuum and non-style. Germany was the country of rational work-intoxication. Yet did the Austrians, the Viennese, work less? Was this really nothing but the roast chicken era, a period of pure hedonism and sheer decoration of life? And, if so, why?

Of course the Austrians worked too, perhaps in somewhat less possessed a way than the Berliners, yet certainly no less than the southern

Germans. Daily life presented the same demands everywhere. Austrian science accomplished no less than German science: Ernst Mach worked in Vienna, and even if his physical-philosophical life's work went unnoticed there, the same would have happened to him in Germany. Vienna was the source of the most important technological innovations (for instance the propeller); but above all Vienna was the seat of a medical school which in a period of development of more than a hundred years — since its foundation under Joseph II — under the direction of men like Van Swieten, Hyrtl, Rokitansky, and finally Billroth, had raised itself to be the foremost in the world.[13] In the light of such achievement one could certainly — just as in Germany — disregard the value vacuum.

Yet the desire was not only to disregard it but also to gloss over it. One played at great art, not as crudely as later under Wilhelm II, to say nothing of the Hitler period, yet still not quite unconsciously, hence not without untruthfulness. Munich designated itself "Athens-on-the-Isar" because within its walls a kind of "neo–Van Dyckism" and "neo–Velazquezism" was practiced (admittedly not by the strong and willful Leibl) and there was even some poetry on the side. Now for all the acknowledgement of the painterly qualities of a Lenbach and even his successor Habermann, or of the literary qualities of his poetic fellow citizen Heyse,[14] "Athens-on-the-Isar" was a farce, in part the effort of Bavarian particularism against Berlin, but in part the farce of an unintended self-directed irony fully approved by the Munich *Fliegende Blätter,* the humorless comic rag of the German burgher of the time. Not for nothing was the word *kitsch* coined in Munich at that time. And yet, involuntary as this self-directed irony may have been, Bavarian

---

[13] Gerard van Swieten (1700–1772); Joseph Hyrtl (1829–94); Carl von Rokitansky (1804–78); Theodor Billroth (1829–94): for detailed treatment of these four physicians and the Vienna Medical School they formed and reformed, see Erna Lesky, *The Vienna Medical School of the Nineteenth Century* (Baltimore: Johns Hopkins University Press, 1976), trans. L. Williams and I. S. Levii, M.D.

[14] Wilhelm Leibl (1844–1900); Franz von Lenbach (1836–1904); Hugo von Habermann (1849–1929); Paul Heyse (1830–1914).

national sarcasm did not leave it in the unconscious but turned it back into the conscious and thereby back into the genuine, and for that very reason "Athens-on-the-Isar" won that humorous veneer which provided the city's peculiar charm, its art, its entire atmosphere.

Although Vienna felt itself just as much an art city, indeed an art city par excellence, its atmosphere was entirely different. It was really far less a city of art than a city of decoration par excellence. In accordance with its decoration, Vienna was cheerful, often idiotically cheerful, but with little sense of indigenous humor or even sarcasm and self-directed irony. As for literary production, aside from the catching feuilletons practically nothing existed. The passing of Stifter and Grillparzer, who had provided Austria's only important contribution to German and hence to world literature, and who were now without successors, touched almost no one. Poetry was an affair of gold-edged books on the parlor table, and for that a Rudolph Baumbach or at best a Friedrich von Halm were the most appropriate.[15] The visual arts, on the other hand, were necessary for the decoration of life, and they were valued according to their usefulness; Viennese decorative art rightly named its non-style after its most representative painter, the beauty-virtuoso Hans Makart. He was the greatest decorator of the epoch, and the epoch became — at least in Vienna — the Makart period. If in Munich the game was "neo–Van Dyck," Makart conjured in his paintings a kind of Rubens opera, to the astonished delight of his contemporaries. In the 1873 Imperial Parade, which he designed, he actually appeared disguised as Rubens, riding a white saddle horse. And all those who, out of artistic honesty, could not or would not conform to the Makart style — for instance the brilliant, often nearly impressionistic experimenter Pettenkofen, or the Viennese *veduto* painter Rudolf von Alt who, though thor-

---

[15.] Rudolf Baumbach (1840–1905); Friedrich von Halm (Baron Münch-Bellinghausen, 1806–71), today a forgotten writer, but at one point a competitor of Grillparzer's.

oughly original, was still frankly reminiscent of Canaletto, or the important painters of Viennese landscape Jacob Schindler and Tina Blau, as well as many others — all were inevitably overshadowed by this kind of high decorative style.[16] But Vienna stood on its "decoration rights," and — this is the essential point — was to a substantial degree entitled to do so, not only because decorativeness was a fundamental characteristic of the epoch, but far more because it had exerted its purest and finest effect in the musical and theatrical tradition of Austria. Dutiful concern for this tradition removed from Viennese decorativeness the farcical spirit with which the Germans — especially in Munich — were trying to gloss over the value vacuum, and if, despite that concern, this decorativeness was far from being granted true legitimacy, the legitimacy it did achieve was more defensible than it could have been anywhere else in Europe.

If anywhere, decorativeness was legitimate in Vienna; only it was more or less that kind of legitimation which befits the establishment and maintenance of a museum. In fulfillment of its duty to tradition, Vienna confused culture with "museumness" *[Museumshaftigkeit]* and became a museum to itself (unfortunately not in its architecture, where it was guilty of the most outrageous devastations). Because Haydn and Mozart, Beethoven and Schubert had miraculously converged on this spot, had been badly treated and had nevertheless composed, Vienna set itself up as a musical institution. Germany never set itself up as a poetic institution, in spite of Weimar, and not even "Athens-on-the-Isar" did anything of the sort with its painting. The "museumish" *[das Museale]* was reserved for Vienna, indeed as a sign of its ruin, the sign of Austrian ruin. For in despondency decay leads to vegetating, but in wealth it leads to the museum. Museumishness *[Musealität]* is the vegetating of wealth, a cheerful vegetating, and Austria was at the time still a wealthy country.

[16.] August von Pettenkofen (1822–89); Rudolf von Alt (1812–1905); Emil Jakob Schindler (1842–92), father of Alma Mahler-Werfel; Tina Blau (1845–1916).

THE Viennese have always felt uneasy with the Germans, especially the northern Germans, and the wish to differentiate themselves from the Germans, even at the price of this museumishness, would probably have always gained their consent. The fact that this museumish posture also distinguished Vienna from Paris, however, would have met with less approval. For Vienna has always been proud of its similarities to Paris.

Clearly the two cities have much in common, mainly in atmosphere. Paris of course was never the explicitly musical city that Vienna was, but it surpassed Vienna, if possible, in its love for the theater. The lightness of the theatrical and the love for the theater, the lightness of the ever present desire for pleasure and entertainment, in short the love of spectacle was innate in the people of both cities, and in each had become the breeding ground for a dominating theater culture through which that love, in turn, was continually reawakened and kept on the move. The Comédie Française and the Vienna Burgtheater were parallel institutions, and their high style had its effect beyond the theater, reaching out as a model into every stratum of the population (not only to the bourgeoisie), setting the pace for language and conduct, and influencing more than ever what remained of the genuine and vital popular theater of both cities, even popular musical comedy, which for its part was still in a state of dependence — part imitative, part satirical-polemical — on grand opera. In no other place was the entire texture of life so tightly interwoven with that of the theater as it was in Paris and Vienna.

Such common interests point to resemblances in national character. But national character is correlated to historical conditions and experiences; each determines the other. During the seventeenth and eighteenth centuries, Paris and Vienna were the power centers of the European continent, and the rivalry between the houses of Bourbon and Habsburg was the axis around which world politics rotated. France and Austria had won exceptional positions within the European balance of power; they had to defend themselves against each other, and thus both required the most highly developed organization in order to accomplish the world-political tasks this situation presented them with. They in fact became the two most modern continental states of the Baroque. This new state organization was centralized — in France even more than in Austria — yet it was unable in the name of this centralization to deny or even to destroy what might be called its natural administrative foundations, which were anchored in feudal and ecclesiastical institutions. Nor could it become tyrannical, since it needed the people and especially the bourgeoisie as a counterweight to the power of the feudal and ecclesiastical lords. The solution to this extremely difficult problem lay in the indigenously Baroque, downright oriental hypertrophy of the courtly. Through the splendor of the court, the minor nobles and collateral lines could be alienated from the great noble families, and through the court it became more and more possible to secularize spiritual and cultural spheres which until that point had been directed exclusively by the clergy — for example, through the foundation of scholarly academies as principally courtly institutions. And if, with all this, the people were seldom assigned anything more than the role of an astonished spectator — a role they had genuinely accepted — they felt themselves becoming more and more of a political factor, and certainly the one as much as the other and even both together were from then on thoroughly calculated to influence decisively the national character. As a participant in the new consciousness of power and splendor, the people of the rival cities Paris and Vienna had become bearers of a common lifestyle. Rivalry and affinity have always been siblings.

The secularization of spiritual life was initiated by Protestantism; thus its imitation in the court also had a religious-political goal, namely, the reconsolidation of Catholicism within the new framework of the state. Art was not the last thing to be affected. Insofar as the bourgeois private intimacy, into which the Protestant secularization process had necessarily to flow, was replaced by the spectator-oriented "amusement of the sovereign" (with the salon providing maximum intimacy), secularization was caught in a domain which for technical reasons alone had to remain practically unattainable for the bourgeois and his artistic pursuits. Grand concerts, grand opera, and above all the theater, all of them removed from the sphere of the private, were antithetical to chamber music and still-life painting, and for that very reason they formed one of those bridges that could bring the people into immediate contact. The tradition from which the Bourbon and Habsburg residences emerged as theater cities began in the two court theaters and always drew new sustenance from them. And there were no Protestant theater cities.

In any case the monarchic-courtly element became more and more superfluous, in other words an empty convention. For every self-solidifying tradition becomes autonomous in the end. The tradition of the Comédie Française has smoothly survived every royal deposition. It would probably have been no different with the Burgtheater; but there was no Austrian revolution — the cleverly timed administrative reforms of Joseph II did more than a little to avoid one, and so courtly convention remained intact for Viennese intellectual life and especially for the theater. Academic life, too, long remained under the protection of an imperial prince; the opera long kept its gala performances, at which the attendance of the emperor transmitted to the spectator a morsel of participation in the luster of divine right. And for a long time the private theaters, officially unvisited by the court and therefore excluded from its luster, maintained — even the smallest of them — a royal box (like the equally unused "royal waiting rooms" in the major railway stations) clearly visible, its plush-red, rather cheap ostentation constantly in the public's eyes, so that pleasure in theater continued to be ordered around the scheme of monarchical value hierarchy. For a truly seeing eye, this continuously unused, continuously dark box clearly had the effect of a museum piece and, indeed, because of this very museumishness, of a symbol of empty convention of monarchical Baroque gesture.

Austria in the nineteenth century had become museumish, not only intellectually but also politically (no organism, at the very least a community where one part conditions the other, contains isolated zones). The path of revolution, which may well have been in the mind of the reformer Joseph II, treads on the razor's edge, the precipice into revolution on its left, that into reaction on its right, and he who would follow it needs an instinct for balance of the type that may have developed only in insularly assured England. Austria, threatened from without and nationally torn from within, possessed nothing of this instinct, could not possess it, and where it did not fall into reaction, it had to become stagnant and museumish. While Paris surmounted its Baroque structure through revolutionary thrusts and so made possible the development of the world city already germinating within it, Vienna remained a Baroque city, far from that passionate gloom and latent revolutionism that is indigenous to every world city, that smoldered beneath the cheerfulness of nineteenth-century France and even today is not extinguished yet could well be extinguished when Paris loses its status as a world city. For an uprising to transcend itself and turn into a revolution — as was the case in France in 1789 — it must achieve a worldwide effect; it must — as became ever clearer in the nineteenth century — strive toward world revolution, and this demands a world center as a stage, at least a potential world city and not just some kind of national metropolis. And Austria, as a country that had partly lost, partly squandered its world-political mission, was utterly unfit to contain such a city. After 1848, the city — its working-class quarter not excepted — moved ever more deeply into the unrevolutionary, the hedonistic, the skeptic-courteous, courteous-skeptic. Vienna became an "un-world city," and, without thereby becoming a small town, it sought small-town tranquillity, small-town narrowmindedness, small-town pleasures, the charm of "once upon a time." It was still a metropolis, but a Baroque metropolis, and one for which there were no more Baroque politics.

At this point, their resemblance in atmosphere notwithstanding, the primary commonality between Paris and Vienna is annulled. A city in an acute value vacuum, a city turned museumish, no longer has anything essential in common with one that finds itself in a stormy value upheaval. And a people turned provincial has a different character from a cosmopolitan people and therefore must also produce a different kind of art. This is immediately visible in popular art. If one compares the three types of operetta embodied in Offenbach, Sullivan, and Johann Strauss, the third — contrary to the first two — lacks any satirical tendency. The ironic note that had distinguished the Viennese popular stage in its classical epoch in the first half of the nineteenth century (the romantic irony of Raimund and the biting irony of Nestroy)[17] had completely disappeared, and nothing remained of it but the totally idiotic counterfeit of comic opera and its sometimes appealing, sometimes insipid romanticism. What was spreading here was the flat cynicism of sheer, i.e., exclusively decorative, amusement, and the adequate carrier of its immorality was the waltz-genius of Strauss. To be sure, comic opera lives also in the satire of Offenbach and the social caricature of Sullivan, and surely these contain almost as genuine an amusement and cynicism, but it is that exceedingly cosmopolitan cynicism whose aggressiveness stems from political aspiration and finds its moral support in such aspiration — an aggressiveness that is for that very reason indispensable to the realization of satire. All this was lost to the Viennese after 1848, so that the operetta form created by Strauss became a specific vacuum-product; yet as a vacuum-decoration it proved itself all too durable, and its later worldwide success can be taken as a *mene-tekel*[18] for the submergence of the whole world into the relentlessly widening value vacuum.

Vienna, center of the European value vacuum — surely a somewhat

---

[17.] Ferdinand Raimund (1790–1836) and Johann Nepomuk Nestroy (1801-62) are generally referred to together as Austria's most famous popular dramatists.

[18.] The words *mene, mene, tekel, upharsin:* the "handwriting on the wall," interpreted by Daniel to mean that God had weighed Belshazzar and his kingdom, had found them wanting, and would destroy them (Daniel 5:25).

absurd honor and distinction, yet not so absurd when one takes into account the sociopolitical texture of the city, the social texture of Austria itself, unique in Europe.

5. THE POLITICAL VACUUM[19]

Of the seven European major powers, France in 1871 had definitely become a republic. The remaining six, still monarchies to be sure, were nevertheless in no way structurally alike. Two of them, Russia and Spain, had held onto an apparently unchanged Baroque political form; that is, they adhered now as before to the monarchical (in Russia also theoretical) centralization of the state established in the seventeenth century, which had cast off the medieval feudal system, had de-autonomized it with the counterweight of the non-noble estates, and had continued nevertheless to use it as an instrument of administration, hence endowing it with its final nature, which has lasted until the most recent times. They were able to do this because their bourgeoisie — still numerically insignificant — was in no position to impose a further shift in equilibrium, and they had to do it, because with the bourgeoisie as weak as it was — a weakness Lenin was the first to perceive as common to both countries — economic and social revolution lurked beneath the numbness of the superannuated state. Conversely, the long solidified bourgeois economic order of the new Italian and German monarchies — *parvenue* and rabble monarchies in aristocratic eyes — needed no such help. Italy could have followed France down the republican path without further ado, and the German empire, this hyperdecorative resuscitation of the now thoroughly Protestant-centered and no longer Roman "Holy Empire," was in the end a Bismarckian trick for the union of

[19.] "The Political Vacuum": subtitle added by Hannah Arendt (her handwritten insertion of the subtitle appears on the manuscript carbon copy she used to edit the 1955 Rhein-Verlag edition of the essay — Hermann Broch Archive, Beinecke Library of Yale University).

German National Liberalism with the Prussian feudalistic *Junkertum,* the trick of a pseudofederalism that camouflaged nothing but Prussian hegemony — the perpetuation of its mastery over Habsburg as over all the constituent German states, which had been conceded shadowlike autonomous existences within the bounds of the empire. The circumstances were completely different, however, in England and Austria: the representative mission of the Victorian as well as of the Francisco-Josephinian monarchy was dictated neither by decorative — let alone hyperdecorative — nor by tricksterish, least of all by economic necessities, but by political necessity.

Behind this nonetheless curious English-Austrian resemblance, analogous causes were at work in both countries, clearly presaging opposite results. (England had been on the rise for two hundred years, Austria in decline.) Notwithstanding the symbolic meaning of the crown — in England as a sign of the everlasting continuity of British power and its growth, in Austria as the expression of the old German, mystically based, imperial glory that had once been experienced and to which one held fast in spirit despite its loss — notwithstanding such emotional impulses, by no means unimportant politically, the crown erected in both places a thoroughly rational, practical, indeed indispensable state-building institution; in the case of Austria it lent a secure, legally tenable unity to the complicated and scattered conglomerate of autonomies and semi-autonomies that formed the Habsburg empire, in the case of England it provided the same for the even more complicated, ever expanding world empire of colonies, dominions, mandates, etc. In both cases, the unifying strength of the crown was a political necessity. Borne by such necessity, the English as much as the Austrian-Baroque monarchy was able to conform to the demands of the times in a more or less constant evolution, without drastic breaks in tradition. (Even the Cromwell interregnum hardly counts as a break in tradition, much less, therefore, a brief reign like the Viennese March revolution of 1848.) In contrast to the still Baroque-feudal monarchies of the German and Italian thrones, only in England and Austria was constitutional monarchy (with great-power status) realized in a "natural" manner.

The "natural," evolutionary constitutionalization of a state fulfills itself as a gradual, step-by-step transfer of crown privileges — above all the authority to set laws — to the sovereignty of the people. Defeat in foreign policy, lost wars, and other emergencies are what generally force the crown to settle for such popularly appeasing concessions. The constitutionalization of Austria in the nineteenth century is an example of this. And the much older English constitutionalization was initiated by the very same causes. But then the picture changes. The more England found the path suited to it — the colonial-imperialist one (and thereby differentiated itself structurally from the continental powers), the more its democratization became the concern of the entire people, and the more it was advanced through foreign success rather than defeat, through welfare rather than distress. Even if the upswing was broken by a political or an economic crisis, the position of the crown became all the more solid, for it was this very upswing that increased its necessity; aware of this, the crown was forced on its own behalf to yield to the wishes of the people. Thus, from the original (fluctuating) three-cornered equilibrium of royal, noble, and bourgeois power, the immediate influence of the throne slowly lost its place, and the weight of the bourgeoisie, which united increasingly with the nobility, was bit by bit replaced by that of the proletariat. Yet, whatever it may have been like, this totally unique power game, comparable to none on the continent, brought on an eminently political result — the conservative-progressive consensus on which English democracy rests, and through which it became exemplary.

Concrete politics, whether good or bad, are made by concrete men, through dictates in a true absolute divine monarchy, through compromise in true democracy. Yet an absolutism compelled into compromise (and wanting still to remain absolute) begins to tack into the wind, and he who wishes to dictate in a democracy (without robbing it of the dem-

ocratic) tacks into the same ambiguous course, even if he is able to justify himself — as is usually predetermined — with the ability to steady
himself on abstract, unshakable dogmas. No abstractly oriented politics, from Plato to Wilson, has developed into politically enduring
action, and as much as tacking may belong to political technique, never,
not even with Franklin D. Roosevelt, has it led to a founding political
idea. Richelieu and Mazarin, with a disregard for all abstract and for that
matter all Catholic principles, practiced concrete absolutist politics,
and England never deviated from the concrete but attached herself to
it all the more tenaciously as she became more democratic. Austrian
or, more precisely, Habsburg politics were from the very beginning
attracted, in a strange combination, to tacking and to the abstract, and
because of that they were later compelled to remain so by virtue of the
relations they had created.

Surely every action attended to by concrete men is concrete; yet that
does not prevent it from mirroring the concrete-abstract discordance of
its motivations. And the Habsburgs were not ones to allow such discordance to be absent. They were endowed to an overwhelming extent
with political instinct, yet one which ultimately focused on the anti-
political. Beneath their extraordinary talent for the Machiavellian, as
well as for every kind of political intrigue and maneuver, lurked often a
lack of determination and the abstract-playful propensity to a tacking
for its own sake, but one that remains fixed to one spot, and for this —
senile and skeletonized — Charles V's ghostlike clock-making mania
offers the clearest evidence. But where the Habsburgs, however rarely,
were truly human and, like Maximilian ("the last knight"), found true
contact with the people, this connection became — as the popular leg-
endary anecdotes about Emperor Max show — a paternalistic, home-
oriented family connection that corresponded to their unpolitical ideal.
The issue was the fear of politicization, the deeply rooted antipathy to
the masses politicized through questions of faith (other causes were at
that time hardly involved), and this fear was so fundamentally corrobo-

rated by the bitter experience of the Thirty Years' War that Jesuitism, already enlisted against the masses in a similar way, came to be granted not only the direction of the Counterreformation but also a decisive influence on the nature of statecraft. Through Jesuitic teaching, Habsburg abstractism wins its theoretical footing, through Jesuitic rules, its tacking becomes methodical and nearly indomitable, through Jesuitic determination, its discordance is raised to the systematic.

These were the weapons with which Habsburg encountered the emerging democratization of the period between 1789 and 1848. Joseph II's famous reforms, sprung from under the shadow of the French Revolution and the threat of its contagion, were an act of Jesuitic schooling and Machiavellian tacking, although Joseph himself — rationalistic and hence dogmatic, politically unconcrete and hence purposive, humanitarian and hence undemocratic, feeble and hence vitreously inflexible, in short a man of utmost coolness and utmost disunion — considered himself a convinced defender of human rights, unaware that in his state-centralized efforts (admittedly not racist) toward Germanization, he simultaneously withheld those rights from the non-German Austrians. Momentary compromises of an absolute ruler, his reforms could be eliminated without further ado at the outbreak of the Napoleonic wars, in which the reforms no longer acted as preventive measures, but rather as fifth-column instruments of French ideas. This happened promptly, brutally, and without success through his successors Leopold II and Franz I; without success, because in the post-Napoleonic period, the peril of Austria and Habsburg was more evident than ever (never yet have the ideas that carried a usurper and that were carried by him been destroyed together with his overthrow). The French danger was replaced by the German one, on one hand in the form of the revitalized Prussian desires for hegemony, on the other in the form of every foolish irredentist democratic movement that longed for a parliamentary Greater Germany; and alongside the latter, no less irredentistically, the centrifugal forces existing in the so-called "nationali-

ties" suddenly revealed themselves — in part of course also as a consequence of the Josephinian campaign of Germanization, not yet it is true
among the Czechs and southern Slavs, but clearly among the Poles
(who refused to get over the fact of their lost kingdom) as well as in
Venetia and Lombardy. And every one of these dangers had necessarily
to abet the strengthening of the intra-Austrian democratic tendencies.
No wonder, then, that under the paternalistic reign of Franz I, who —
similarly cool but essentially more straightforward than Joseph II and,
in compensation, equipped with a certain underhanded wit —
sought, partly through exhortation, partly through malice, to bring his
subjects to reason, the "secret ones," as the Austrian state police[20] of
the time were popularly designated, became omnipotent, the censors
continuously gained in harshness, and the notorious Spielberg Prisons
became even fuller of "political" prisoners. For what went on here in the
form of aggressive Metternichian radical conservatism (in domestic as
well as foreign politics) was more than mere reaction. Not one of those
concerned — not even Gentz or even Adam Müller,[21] although they
saw most clearly through this conservatism — saw that the Counterreformation, in an immense final effort, had become completely political and, according to its mission, was making a final attempt to rescue
the integrity of the Austrian state through radical depoliticization.

[20.] Broch's original manuscript had read "Austrian F.B.I." instead of "Austrian state
police."

[21.] Friedrich von Gentz (1764–1832) and Adam Heinrich Müller, Ritter von Nitterdorf
(1779–1829), statesmen and political philosophers. Among Gentz's writings translated
into English: *Origins and Principles of the American Revolution Compared with the
Origins and Principles of the French Revolution,* trans. John Quincy Adams (Delmar,
N.Y.: Scholars' Facsimile, 1977); *Reflections on the Liberty of the Press in Great Britain*
(London, 1820); *On the State of Europe before and after the French Revolution*
(London, 1803). See Golo Mann, *Secretary of Europe: The Life of Friedrich von Gentz,
Enemy of Napoleon,* trans. William H. Woglom (London: Oxford University Press,
1946). On Adam Müller, see Desider Vikor, *Economic Romanticism in the Nineteenth
Century* (New Delhi: New Book Society of India, 1964). The correspondence between
Gentz and Müller is available in German (Briefwechsel zwischen Friedrich Gentz und
Adam Müller [Stuttgart: J. G. Cotter, 1857]).

Eighteen forty-eight made it clear that this effort had become futile. When Ferdinand I, the most harmless of tyrants who always softened in the face of revolution, abdicated and with the historic words "All right, Frankie, be good" ("Schon recht, Franzl, bleib brav"), handed over the imperial command to his eighteen-year-old nephew Franz Joseph I, he handed over at the same time an empire that no longer was an empire, in other words a state already rejected by the overwhelming majority of its population. For all the proletarian participation, this was clearly a predominantly bourgeois revolution, loyal to the emperor and hence one in which the typically bourgeois freedoms of constitutionalism were demanded; it was also an Austrian revolution and hence affirmed Austria and desired its continuance. For even if the intellectuals and students, the spiritual leaders of this revolution, were in many ways opposed to their predominantly Catholic fathers, they were still, like them, rooted in their home institutions, partly through class interest and partly through romantic sentiment, and they knew, at least they suspected, that without the unifying crown of the Habsburgs the state structure would crumble. Their dream was Austrian freedom, a freedom with which they hoped to gather the separately struggling nationalities back to a new Austrian unity, and they did not consider the fact that in the majority of the provincial cities even their own linguistic and class contemporaries were already infected by irredentism and panGermanism, and, indeed, that the revolutionary sympathies of these contemporaries, not to mention those of the nationalities, were not striving for state consolidation, but for the accelerated destruction of the state. In its illusions about Austria, the Viennese revolution was just as abstract as the regime it battled, yet in the unleashing of the centrifugal forces of the nationalities – the very fear Metternich had held for forty years – it was concrete; it was the most concrete of dangers.

Fundamentally, this was already the dissolution of the Austrian state, even if for the time being it revealed itself only as a paradoxical situation. Even if the young, inexperienced emperor had had the finest democratizing intentions, the partiality of the Viennese revolution would have prevented him from finding a point of departure for them. For to democracy — as is the case in England — there belongs a total population prepared to be responsible to the state, whereas here the majority of the population was at most prepared to live within the state as a responsibility-free, yet respected, in any case grumbling guest, and to wait for the opportunity to destroy it. Aside from the Viennese *Bürgertum,* revolutionary-liberal as well as Catholic, devotion to Austria was extant only among the resident peasantry of the (German Alpine) "hereditary lands" *[Erblanden];* for them, loyalty to the emperor was a purely mystical tradition maintained in the depths of their being, surpassing everything political (the similarly disposed Croatia stood under Hungarian dominion); and, even if one takes into account the splinter groups of great-agrarian and feudal type whose adherence to the state, regardless of nationality, depended above all on the guarantee of their special position — even then, hardly an eighth of the population, hence a vanishing, tiny segment, could be regarded as a life-carrying substance of the state. Eighteen forty-eight made it unequivocally clear that, without the crown, the Austrian structure was absolutely void of substance; that concentrated within the crown was the state's entire principle of inertia — the most important requisite for its existence; in short, that the crown alone represented the substance of the state. A kind of totality function was incumbent on the crown, a kind of involuntary "L'État c'est moi," and if this expression had actually been as proud in the mouth of Franz Joseph as it had been in the mouth of Louis XIV, it would have been a cry of despair.

In other words, whereas the politically unifying function of the crown is compatible with constitutionalism and democracy, as the English example shows, its totality function — no less necessary for Austria — craved absolutism in an almost terrifying way. The relapse into the old regime, inaugurated with the Schwarzenberg ministry, was upbraided for its counterrevolutionary vindictiveness; actually it was a solution to a difficult predicament and owed its astonishing decade-long lifespan to the equally astonishing foreign political successes of the anti-Prussian course of the time. Yet after the triumphant defeat of 1859 (defeat in war after victory in battles had become Austria's lot), after the cession of Lombardy and Venetia to the newly unified Italy, a major change in course could no longer be avoided. Schmerling, who as a liberal had led the Austrian union in the 1848 Frankfurt parliament, was called to the government in place of Schwarzenberg, and in 1861 the emperor established the first pan-Austrian parliament. The Austrian constitution was born, much later of course than the English one and determined by a completely different state structure; yet, like the English constitution, it was the final, necessary phase in the steady development of a monarchical tradition unbroken since the Middle Ages and the Baroque.

Austria had entered the closing phase of its existence as a state, and it could well be that Franz Joseph, who in the meantime had grown to manhood, had such premonitions as he drove along the debris of Vienna's now demolished city walls, over the still undeveloped glacis – where the Ringstrasse would later arise – to the provisional wooden houses of the new Parliament in front of the Schottentor, to open its first session. It was a parliamentary assembly by means of which government was still possible; a subtly crafted class suffrage guaranteed unconditional majority to the loyal Austrian party led by German liberals, and thus pressed the "nationalities," despite their popular majority, into a helpless minority and confined their centrifugal forces, at least in terms of legislating capacity. By this time, it is true, voices had already been raised – not least from the ranks of the nationalities – demanding the initiative of a "just," federative parliamentary system, but how could that have been brought about? The mere attempt to establish it had fired disputes to the boiling point among the kaleidoscopic overlapping settlements of the nationality groups, and it had justifiably to be accepted that their counterachievement of "repatriotization" (the very expectation of the revolutionary idealists of 1848) would become more than insecure. It seemed absolutely impossible to create a federative "justice," and in its place there emerged almost necessarily the peculiarly Habsburgian system of political preferences, a system which — clearly at the price of discrimination against Austria by Hungary's special position — understood actually how to make weakness into strength through a Machiavellian exploitation of the nationality dispute. In other words, it turned the centrifugal mechanism into a kind of equilibrium, or at least imposed on it a temporary suspension of the problem. It was a process of constant "tacking" and of more or less official reforming, of constant negotiating both inside and outside Parliament (mostly the latter). But it led the way to 1873, and indeed, in a whirl of revolutionary tendencies and temperaments, which at every external loss of power threatened to flare up to double the danger, it led Austria to a final heyday which — even if it was only a false heyday — reached into the twentieth century and became the swan song of Vienna.

But this was a heyday of an abstract structure. The more vocal the nationalities became, by dint of the ever growing concessions which they had forced — the preference system had a purely retarding effect — the more Austria disappeared. The German minority, until now loyal to the state, robbed of its preferred position and hence embittered, degenerated altogether to a pan-German irredenta of sheer pre-Hitlerian character. Its place was filled by the Christian Socialist party of Lueger, later mayor of Vienna. Under a Catholic banner, yet with a demagogic employment of pre-Hitlerian methods, he had once again, if through a different stratification, gathered the imperially loyal elements, first of all the Viennese petite bourgeoisie and then, with the aid of the clergy, the Alpine peasantry, and from this tradition-bound, indeed democratic basis — the same occurred in Hungary from a Croatian basis — he intended not only to reinstate the situation of 1850 together with its reactionary course but also to convert the nationalities to that course and thus resolve their problematic through a kind of intra-Austrian Catholic International. The latter was a goal modeled on that of the rapidly growing Workers' Party, which likewise presumed it would be able to engender an intra-Austrian International bridging all nationality quarrels, just as long as it were granted equal, direct, and universal suffrage. The nationalities did support the demand, but when suffrage was achieved, they did not adopt the tendencies of the two Internationals to preserve the state. The centrifugal forces remained untamed, indeed were becoming constantly more untamable, and began to wear away the structure of the state with increasing speed so that the parliamentary machinery, which surrendered the stage to this — allegedly toward the goal of an Austrian legislation — became a specter of its own goal. What subsisted of the Austrian state was the specterlike skeleton of a theory in which no one any longer believed.

The state was one thing, and the political machinery existing inside it quite another; between the two lay a kind of impenetrable insulating layer, at which apparently both of these became abstract. Just as Machiavellianism is in itself mere political technique and as such not politics, so parliamentary rules of procedure, for all the ardor of the battles waged within their boundaries, are far from being democracy, because democracy goes hand in hand with democratic consensus and democratic compromise, and these in turn go hand in hand with the state together with the common weal for whose sake compromises are sealed. Here, however, in a rejected state, in the state vacuum, non-democracy reigned, and the only thing it still shared with more genuine democracy was the overcoming of absolutism. Step by step, in an almost never explicit, tacking, retreat operation, Franz Joseph had given up the last bits of absolutism that remained to him. Yet not only does every strategy that merely masters retreat, that is in itself, so to speak, a retreat strategy, inevitably become abstract in the end; in this case it had to become all the more abstract as it drifted more and more, in the final third of the century, into the state vacuum and hence to the spot where all concreteness is extinguished. And so it happened. The Machiavellian perfidy of the early Habsburgs (even if Austrian abstractness was already

pronounced under Joseph II) was a lively concreteness in contrast to
the correct bureaucratism by which Franz Joseph I ran his government
operations, never overstepping the constitutional boundaries which he
had once accepted. Precisely because the substance of the state was ever
more acutely reduced to the crown, and because the subsisting remains
of the state became ever more identical to the crown, the remarkably
vacuumlike character of the state had likewise to be taken over by the
crown. The discordance of a constitutional state in which "L'État c'est
moi" is still to have value – albeit only as substance, yet for this reason
no less absurdly – also impinges on the "moi." Thus the crown became
as abstract an institution as the state it embodied, and the insular layer
which severed the state from the events happening within it surrounded
the crown now more than ever.

   The older Franz Joseph I grew, the more he immersed himself in the
vacuum of his vocation and the more identical he felt with the state,
whose fatal destiny was tied to his own, and whose insulated abstractness he was thus forced to carry. Habsburgian in his sense of coolly
unapproachable, hierarchical dignity – his most conspicuous characteristic – he drew from this situation a single corresponding consequence, namely, absolute seclusion. He had never been paternalistic –
for that he had acceded to the throne too young; yet now men no longer
valued him, and his existence became hermetic. They had all betrayed
Austria in compelling him toward such calamitous political advance-
ment; even his own son – no doubt a crucial trauma – had allied himself
with them, and thus the apaternal raised itself into the antipaternal, dis-
claiming humanity altogether. Whether commoners, nobles, or princes
of the royal house, all of them were empire spoilers searching for reform,
an undistinguishable mass, a world of variability before which he,
monarch and guardian of imperial subsistence, was compelled to retreat
into the immutable. Every reform, every technical invention no matter
how insignificant, every modernization of life – whether an automobile,
a bathroom, or a wardrobe – that was not allowed in the imperial

palaces, became for him a symbol and a symptom of those forces that had brought Austria to the edge of the precipice. He opposed new buildings in the city (for example on the Mariahilferstrasse, through which he rode day after day from Schönbrunn to the "castle"), and his former consent to the demolition of the Vienna city walls and thus the destruction of the old city plan must have haunted him all his life as a sin of youth fraught with the gravest consequences. Surely such an extreme penchant for the immutable can be looked upon as senile, as the private court ceremony of an imperial senile old man, perhaps even as the devious private magic of a helpless creature; all the same, dignity prevailed. It was the immutability of an invisible and undefined imprisonment in which he had found himself drawn into a seclusion infinitely more bitter than that of the Vatican because it proceeded in a vacuum and its stubbornness was that of a solitude that reached out far beyond the individual. Immense was the shell of solitude in which he lived his uncannily bureaucratic, abstractly punctual official life, no matter whether in the Vienna "castle" or in the simple Biedermeier villa at Ischl where annual hunting vacations took him, always in abstract exactness, always in solitude, always in dignity. Wilhelm I was called the first soldier of his empire, Edward VII was the first gentleman of Europe, Franz Joseph I was the abstract monarch par excellence.

And this was exactly the effect he had on his subjects, on the archdukes no less than on the nobles and the burghers and even the working class — this was the effect. He, a man of very meager proportions, a Habsburg who revealed in small measure the inherited qualities of that breed, thus a man with little sense for political and social happenings, yet without immediate access to his fellow man, above all because he lacked any kind of humor and most of all the Habsburg wittiness, in short a truly visionless, narrow, and small-dimensioned man, he was able all the same to become the essence of majesty, in a different way from Louis XIV, it is true, yet with no narrower significance. And this did not occur because a sheer Greek-tragic excess of personal misfortune weighed upon him, neither did it occur from the awe-inspiring effect of such misfortune — this kind of awe-inspired compassion simply disappears from view when the masses are not a public and therefore know no compassion — but it occurred because, perhaps even as a result of all his deficiencies, he had become capable of taking upon himself the thrilling dignity of absolute solitude. For thrill is constantly and instantly extant in the world, and it lurks in every human heart. And so he was seen. He was the opposite of a people's emperor and nevertheless "the" emperor in the eyes of the people.

6. Sociology of the Gay Apocalypse[22]

In accordance with its still predominantly monarchically determined political structure, the European social picture of the nineteenth century — the French republic not excepted — was of a predominantly feudal color. Clearly it was only a tint, a surface, but aristocratic society was still "the" society and for that very reason international. Its life forms were generally the same everywhere; all over Europe there were castles and social exclusivity, hunts and races, and everywhere the nobility was entitled to participate in the court hierarchy that every monarchical head of state was obliged to maintain. Beyond the court, the hierarchy extended to government appointments, to the leading diplomatic and military posts as well as those in internal administrative service, so that out of spite the facade of the state aristocracy — even in France — remained seemingly untouched by all democratic hostility. It had the resistance energy of an autonomous tradition, all the more so when this tradition, having a kind of "natural" affinity with the monarchical tradition, shared an even closer affinity with the state tradition. Historically and economically, feudalism emerged as a result of the possession of the prevailing part of all national power by the nobility (who became nobil-

[22.] "Sociology of the Gay Apocalypse": subtitle presumably added by Hannah Arendt as well (see note 18).

ity in just this way). And since even Baroque monarchy, although it broke feudal autonomy, changed nothing in this respect, it became the charge of the state and a branch of its tradition to protect the possessions of the noble class and guarantee its poor relations, in particular "younger sons," positions appropriate to their rank. The nobility (especially when it grew poor as a consequence of the rise of the bourgeoisie) grew loyal to the state, and for all its antipathy toward the usurping monarchical institution, it used the monarchy in its pact with the state, indeed as an agency, which it then reimbursed with the required court attendance. (The despised "parvenu" monarchies of Germany and Italy also profited from this.) But the pact was always with the state, never with the crown; hence the disappearance of the French crown could be accepted: monarchical tradition is in fact younger than feudal tradition, and the case of France made it clear that it is also shorter-lived.

In any case, the steady, sociologically "natural" relationship between monarchical institution and feudal upper class that unquestionably exists can be understood as follows: where the upper class is despised as the bearer of economic and political oppression — as in Russia and Spain, but equally, for example, in Hungary — the crown is also imperiled; where, however, on account of a lack of tradition the monarchy is insufficiently developed, as in Germany and Italy, the nobility loses the ground from under its feet. And in France, where the throne has been definitely brought down, the upper class — although it still functions as such — has necessarily been reduced to a shadow. Yet to whatever extent the monarchy enjoys political affirmation — in England by the entire population, in Austria by the populations of Vienna and the "hereditary lands," the nobility belonging to it is also affirmed. The Victorian and Francisco-Josephinian nobilities were "popular," more popular by far than the bourgeoisie of the same period, which was becoming evermore suspect; and where an upper class gains popularity, its manner of living sets the trend for all the other classes. They all adopted — with mainly quantitative variations — a common "lifestyle," in England that of the "gentleman," in Austria that of the "cavalier" (both debonair, but in the Protestant-Catholic polarity); and since a common lifestyle represents the "most natural," the most naturally engendered sociological affinity, the crown was to a certain extent included in that sphere.

One could almost speak of a style-democracy. For example, the fact that races organized by jockey clubs — aristocratically exclusive all through Europe — were generally accessible certainly did not make them into democratic institutions. At Longchamps they were a fashion show; in Grünewald, Karlshorst, and Hamburg they were predominantly plebeian betting grounds; yet the fact that at Epsom Downs and at the Vienna Freudenau they took on the character of folk festivals, in which every class up to the court participated equally, gave them, like any other folk festival, a democratic hue. And a similar thing held good for the English and Austrian noble classes themselves. Since they were not under attack, they had no reason to be arrogant, in contrast to their other class contemporaries, the *Junkers* for example. As to the Austrian nobility, which far more than the English had always been tied to the land — this popular affinity was even revealed in the language. The Austrian aristocratic language is indeed "high German" and, moreover, frequently Frenchified, yet it is rooted in dialect and is itself very nearly normalized as pure dialect. Hofmannsthal (his purpose of dramatic characterization notwithstanding) may be said to have been "linguistically entitled" to let Baron Ochs auf Lerchenau of *Der Rosenkavalier* speak in pure popular dialect; and since linguistic normalization is a social mirror, it also became clear that, in closeness to the people, the aristocracy considerably outflanked the burghers, whose touches of dialect continued to fluctuate. Clearly the gentleman and the cavalier were class-conscious nonetheless; clearly they understood each other best in terms of their proficiency at horsemanship and hunting, where they were both unsurpassable, yet the unaffectedness of their democratic attitude played an equal role in this kind of understanding.

Still, for all the affinity between the English and Austrian aristocracies, many things must be taken as opposite omens — as was the case in the comparison of the two monarchies. The English rise and the Austrian decline, the total politics of the English democracy and the non-politics of the Austrian vacuum — this contrast had to have an effect on the status and habits of both noble classes. In England, the pact between state and nobility had become brittle, for the democratic consensus had upset the relationship. Public appointments were no longer made under the influence of the court and its officials, but were used rather (side by side with plutocracy) as a reservoir for the replenishing of the court nobility. Conformity to the new relationships and a corresponding productivity was thus the sole means by which the old nobility could hope to maintain its status as ruling upper class, and their success in doing so was due to the strength of character with which they demonstrated their zeal for the state, and to a maximum of political schooling. Not so in Austria; here the state had to maintain the pact and elicit support from the feudal class as an accessory to the court, all the more so as the feudal class alone was indifferent to nationalities and its members were thus the primary candidates for public positions, to which — in view of the jealous nationalities — the German *Bürgertum,* even if it had remained partially loyal to the state, could be admitted only in limited quantities. Thus without any special effort, governmental prerogative fell to the aristocracy, and when its Hungarian branch continued to fill a slew of important offices, above all in foreign service (profiting from the "Compromise" of 1867), and to exploit these toward securing the Hungarian class-state, with great adroitness, the Austrian in turn needed for his task a minimum of schooling and strength of character, simply because no one demanded anything more. Of course the main difference between the noble classes of England and Austria lay one level deeper: the English believed in their state; the Austrians had no point of reference to justify such faith.

For the Austrian nobility, with its existence bound to that of the state and thereby to that of the crown, could merely participate in the crown's political rearguard actions; and, like the crown, it knew where the path was leading even if it did not generally acknowledge it. No strength of character, no political schooling could have done anything to change that; yet was it necessary for the entire noble class to follow the example of Franz Joseph I and persist in heroic solitude? The nobility chose the lesser, more humanly natural path. Like the Parisian aristocratic society of the Rococo (the resemblance between the false Baroque of the nineteenth century and the genuine Baroque of the eighteenth cannot be denied here), the Austrian nobility was driven by a sense of decline to the most ephemeral pursuit of pleasure. Thus, where the English-Austrian resemblance breaks off, the French-Austrian resemblance begins. And even if the range of comparison was in both cases relatively meager, the Viennese were proud of and happy in the one as well as the other: they loved the solid, anglicizing elegance of their aristocracy; they loved the lighthearted atmosphere of their city, reminiscent of Paris, which the aristocracy kept in motion. And even while sensing the approaching downfall (the portrait of the lonely emperor was his contribution to that), for those who through inherited rank and property were in any case accustomed to the light sense of lightheartedness, the flight into the unpolitical was only right. Whether it was a question of Lueger, of a workers' movement, even if they themselves happened to be involved, they understood the cavalier who would not take it seriously, indeed they were even somewhat ashamed of their own behavior, and the political clamor of others, above all of the "nationalities," struck them as a fundamentally comic and senseless grotesque.

The attitude of the political being has much in common with that of the ethical being. Both would improve the world or at least the state, and in this capacity both want to persuade, educate, and if necessary coerce their fellow man to fixed values which they have determined. The scheme remains the same, no matter if composed of ethical, anethical, or even criminally antiethical politics (like those of Hitler); politics and ethics are structurally the same in their activities. Their affinity reveals itself not least in their ultimately consistently hostile relations to the aesthetic. The strict ethicist, the pure ethicist — Savonarola, Calvin — sees in the aesthetic nothing but the work of the devil, nothing but seduction toward a pursuit of pleasure, the dissuasion of man from his ethical duties, to the extent that it all must be cleared from the field of view in a holy iconoclasm. And if the politician does not go so far in theory, he does so in practice nonetheless. This is true as soon as politics, in the final analysis, achieves mastery, and — whether in domestic or foreign warfare — tramples down any aesthetic human creation. Conversely, where political thought is entirely lacking, either because it has not yet developed or because it has been stunted, the aesthetic category moves more and more into the foreground, and, notwithstanding the exceptional cases in which it evolves into truly artistic production, it generates more and more the tendency toward the ornamentation and decoration of life, culminating in a form of ethical indifference — the counterpart of iconoclasm — that expresses itself as naked hedonism, naked pleasure seeking. There is no doubt that Vienna, having become politically incapable, contributed to such a condition.

The lifestyle of the aristocratic upper class was already in this state; Vienna's swan song of the final third of the century had advanced it, and now it advanced its imitation as well. What the Jesuit Counterreformation and the Jesuitically schooled Habsburg politics, culminating with Metternich prior to 1848, had unsuccessfully striven for for centuries — namely, the attainment whenever possible of a depoliticized, homogenous, harmless pan-Austrian population mass, devoted to a simple pursuit of pleasure and its peaceful aesthetic values — was suddenly realized, belatedly and uselessly, in Vienna and its surroundings. From archduke to folk singer, but also from the *Grossbürgertum* down through the proletariat, the hedonistic attitude prevailed. It was the basis of that particular "style-democracy" that united the nobility with the people, guaranteed their mutual understanding — while still maintaining social distinctions — and made it into that very specifically Austrian *gemütlich* familiarity. Of course this cavalier-conditioned "style-democracy" was markedly different from that of the English gentleman, behind which the genuine political democracy of his country was at work. Austrian social structure had absolutely nothing to do with political democracy. As the product of Austrian vacuousness, in which no one could take anyone seriously because, aside from the national substance of the crown, there was nothing to be taken seriously, the social structure too lost substance and became a sort of gelatin democracy *[Gallert-Demokratie],* in which, when it came right down to it, counts took on the allure of coachmen and coachmen the allure of counts.[23] It was a state of social suspension (for Austria the most adequate right from the beginning) and it was able to be so because the reigning heyday held everything in suspension.

If anywhere, a stateless society was realized here, not merely because, aristocratic and aristocratizing as it was, it constantly peered beyond national boundaries into the international, but, much more so, because these boundaries enclosed an abstraction rather than a state. Yet this abstraction was still a state or, at least, a piece of functional state machinery, and for better or for worse the machinery was attended to by the society which belonged to it, no matter how stateless that society may have been; otherwise it would not have continued to function. In other words, with its existence contingent on the continued existence of Austria, this society, together with its upper class, despite its partly aestheticizing, partly fatalistic hedonism, was in no way ready for suicide and was thus obliged, willingly or not, to submit to a minimum of political thought and political ethics. Yet where were the necessary guiding values? There are aesthetically advanced cultures — and Vienna assuredly did not belong to these — in which a sound political-ethical value system (for example, that of the medieval church or of French Baroque absolutism) achieves such a degree of self-evidence that it

[23.] Broch's use of the terms coachmen *(Fiaker)* and counts *(Grafen)* is an allusion to Hofmannsthal's play *Der Fiaker als Graf (The Coachman as Count).*

grants the aesthetic program which is incorporated in it every liberty to unfold itself. There are also aestheticizing decadent cultures, the stages of degeneration of most great empires since antiquity, which for lack of any indigenous ethical center are forced to allow their most vital foundations to be dictated by an "external" or in some other way "higher" ethical authority. Austria, undoubtedly belonging to this second category, was forced to seek its value orientation where its only substance existed, i.e., in that unifying function of the monarchy which (quite uniquely) fell to the Austrian crown and locked within itself the crown's political as well as its ethical authority (the latter supported by the solitude and the Catholicity of the emperor). It was a social authority, and as such — not as a political authority, which had strayed into a void — it was impressive; indeed, its ethics became sacrosanct and utterly mystical, since rational-skeptical frivolity felt itself obliged to accept them.

And it was all the more mystical when a mere glance at the emperor, and an empty glance at that, represented ethical profit. For the ethical substratum that was mediated there was thoroughly eclectic, and thus truly meaningless. The epoch was eclectic in its ethics as in its aesthetics. The fact that purely ethically oriented communities (contrary to the purely aesthetic orientation), for example those of the Puritans, Calvinists, or Jews, were during their ethical prime aesthetically unproductive and, insofar as they did not altogether reject aesthetic values, accepted them eclectically from external authorities, does not imply that aesthetic eclecticism must have an ethical background. And if Franz Joseph I (mainly as a result of his want of humanity) opposed blindly and obtusely the aesthetic phenomenon and in so doing resembled the genuinely ethical personality, he was nonetheless, despite his ethos of solitude, nothing of the sort. It was no concern of his if the ethical values for which he lived were eclectic, for he accepted them dogmatically, and the aesthetic eclecticism all around him concerned him even less, for he did not notice it at all. And still it turned out that a glance at this mediocrity could give to the Austrian the ballast of social authority — presumably incomprehensible to an Englishman, were he to compare it to his sentiments at the sight of the queen. Yet the eclectic values, not only ethical but also aesthetic values, did undergo an extraordinary invigoration through the mere existence of the imperial old man. In the technical realm of civilization, his inclination to changelessness could not hold life up, but in the far less compelling ethical-aesthetic sphere his conservatism set the trend, because a community that finds itself in decline, and in such a beautiful decline at that, will much sooner follow mystical inclinations than revolutionary ones.

This sort of ethical-aesthetic tie to the crown achieved its clearest expression among the Viennese burghers, to the extent that they were not over-politicized by pan-German and Christian Socialist elements. The Viennese tradesmen, the Viennese industrialists, the Viennese "purveyors to the court," the Viennese faculty members, the Viennese judges, and the Viennese attorneys — all were related to the well-known figure of the Austrian "privy councillor" *[Hofrat],* and, just as politics was forbidden to the Austrian officer, who often sprang from these ranks, they forbade themselves politics. Their political conviction was simply "loyalty to Austria." Because they thought and acted in a manner truly ethical to the state (if not politically), the head of the state, despite its abstractness, was for them an ever surviving, living point of orientation onto which they projected their entire sense of value and from which they extracted all their values. They were a happy mixture of tranquil industriousness and nimbly hedonistic pleasure-seeking, not totally ethical, not totally aesthetic, inwardly steady enough, yet in their judgments in need of corroboration. Neither totally individualistic nor totally collectivist in essence, they were first and foremost a public, the public of the court theater, the court museums, and the concerts and art exhibitions under the court's patronage. Their understanding of art was highly developed, yet unable to deviate an inch from the aforementioned eclectic artistic tradition, and was thus focused exclusively on the virtuoso — on the actor, not the play; on the musician, not the music. All the same, they possessed in the imperial Burgtheater an art in which the eclectic was elevated to originality, the purely aesthetic to the purely ethical. And they were well aware of that, these burghers.

There is no doubt that, apart from the burghers, who were loyal to the emperor and to Austria and representative of a very minor cross section of Austrian society as a whole, things had not changed much. Only that here, where the nobility alone set the trend, respect for the courtly was lacking. For feudalism, which for three hundred years had been pouting at the crown and was still flaunting its former, superior, and more venerable dominion, regarded the monarch at best as primus inter pares and had respect only for itself. Disrespectfulness, however, was no less a fundamental attitude, for that matter an exceedingly un-German fundamental attitude, of the Viennese populace; it belonged solidly to the heritage of the Romance and Slavic influences which were constituent parts of "Austrianness," perhaps the final remains — now of course depoliticized — of a once indisputably extant revolutionism. In this disrespectfulness the populace and the nobility found themselves in the happiest community; indeed they instantly formed the putty for their classless society, the putty-gelatin of their gelatin democracy. And in this sense Franz Joseph I was right after all to lump them all together and keep them without exception at a distance. They all shared the utmost hostility toward him. Yet this grumbling hostility was the single somehow politically colored resistance remaining in this disrespectfulness. Thus the resistance had no effect, not even in the aesthetic. The conditions had become too depoliticized, too lacking in substance, to allow even the slightest movement toward revolution, even toward satire. The farthest any such movement went was the travestying and frivolizing of the courtly values and their ethical-aesthetic content, now appropriated by the burghers; it went as far as the world of the waltz. And precisely because the values which granted some kind of solidity to this society had their origin beyond the insulating layer of the emperor, in the abstraction of the crown, precisely because they aroused at once high and low esteem, horror and confidence, they were not taken seriously, and, through such intensified lack of seriousness, Viennese frivolity maintained that peculiar note which set it apart from any other major city: the note of nonaggression, the note of its utterly mixed-up lightheartedness, amiability, and *Gemütlichkeit*. No doubt there was a measure of wisdom in all this — *Gemütlichkeit* and wisdom blossom in close proximity, the wisdom of a soul that senses demise and accepts it. Nevertheless, it was operetta wisdom, and under the shadow of the approaching demise it became spirited and developed into Vienna's gay apocalypse.

The ultimate meaning of poverty masked by wealth became clearer in Vienna, in Vienna's spirited swan song, than in any other place or time. A minimum of ethical values was to be masked by a maximum of aesthetic values, which themselves no longer existed. They could no longer exist, because an aesthetic value that does not spring from an ethical foundation is its own opposite — kitsch. And as the metropolis of kitsch, Vienna also became the metropolis of the value vacuum of the epoch.